Ed Ginn
2015

SIMPLIFIED PROFITABILITY

Volume 1
Organization Responsibility Centers
Cost Accounting & Profitability

Edward B. Ginn, PE
with Tom Gerry

Activity Based

A knAct, LLC Publication

knAct, LLC
POB 916301., Longwood, FL 32791

+1(1)407.920.8357

www.SimplifiedProfitability.com

Simplified Profitability
Volume 1
Organization Responsibility Centers
Cost Accounting & Profitability

ISBN 978-0-9884746-0-4

My thanks to my wife, Sharon, for her patience and support during the writing of this book and my consulting activities. She is truly my best friend. I could not have accomplished my goals without her.

I also thank my business partner and friend, Tom Gerry. He not only contributed content, he added organization to the book and the process. He is a great sounding board and helped significantly in bringing to fruition a book about a passion of mine.

This book is dedicated to the Glory of God.

Ed Ginn

Contents

Activity Based

www.SimplifiedProfitability.com

Preface

What struck me 30 years ago about Ed's approach is still true today, but advanced with three decades of refinements from hundreds of community financial institutions projects. I convinced my company at that time to hire Resource Management Associates to help us produce results fast.

Since that first experience, I have seen him produce fast, practical results for many financial institutions across the US. I have also been able to work directly with Ed on bank projects in recent years. Here are my observations of his unique tools and techniques, and how Ed brings out the best of everyone that gets involved in the engagements.

RMA focuses on management information and decision making through deeper understanding of business and customer activity drivers. This is a very different purpose than Regulatory and External Reporting. External requirements are critically important and dictate the primary information and accounting design in financial institutions, but, unfortunately, accurate and compliant information for regulatory reporting and the SEC are insufficient for managing a financial institution.

Too often, decisions based just on external reporting lead to actions that do not improve performance, or worse, that decrease profitability and customer satisfaction. RMA helps build bridges to let you use the foundation you are required to have, but then transform current data into effective management information.

Ed is a licensed Industrial Engineer with broad experience in manufacturing, retail and service sectors as well as in financial institutions. He has applied simple, yet powerful, engineering tools to performance improvement in banks. The techniques are easily taught and eminently practical, and the skills learned during an RMA project are reusable.

Financial institutions gain new metrics that are both powerful and simple to explain and understand from the front line, the back office, and all the way up to the Board of Directors. The path from the simple high level measures back through the RMA models all the way to the existing source data is easy to follow.

RMA cost accounting leads to total, fully burdened, and incremental profitability analysis with one consistent framework and presentation, including Organization, Product, Customer, and Relationships. The RMA models are supported with a basic sources data warehouse so RMA can help with any existing systems. Happily, this produces quick results and is a base for continual improvement.

His focus on actual, easy to understand profitability is strikingly similar to the Lean accounting examples in the book, *The Lean Turnaround,* by Art Byrne. Art's book is about the revolution in manufacturing, but he makes a strong case for common sense performance management in service industries as well. Ed Ginn has achieved this in financial institutions.

Ed balances to GL within a small variance percentage without the crutch of any artificial accounts. In my banking days we called those 'Plug' or 'Force Balance' accounts.

This single, consistent approach is useful for a wide range of decisions for tangible profit improvement:

Target costing

Branch rationalization

Capacity planning

Productivity improvement

Outsource vs. in-house comparison

Current vs. alternative technology selection

Marginal pricing analysis

Relationship pricing

In the end, the great advantage of learning and applying RMA tools and techniques comes with flexible and fast results. You will find in this book step-by-step processes and education for cross-functional teams used to fast-track success – three to six months for most projects instead of the industry conventional practices that can take nine months to a year, or longer.

Tom Gerry

AUTHORS

Edward B. Ginn, PE.

Mr. Ginn graduated from the Georgia Institute of Technology, School of Industrial and Systems Engineering. Studies there included cost accounting, work measurement, and capital equipment replacement, among other topics.

Mr. Ginn is a Registered Professional Industrial and Systems Engineer in the state of Georgia (#5874) and the state of Florida (#15288). This requires similar rigid qualifications as a CPA or a member of the bar.

Mr. Ginn served as Engineering Manager in two manufacturing companies and was responsible for the labor and material standards as well as variance analysis within a standard cost system.

Upon entering banking in 1974 he developed one of the first cost accounting systems for data processing and technology. He employed capital equipment replacement techniques for acquisition and modernization of major software.

As a consultant, he designed, developed and installed a profitability analysis system for organization profitability, product profitability and customer profitability in over 30 banks. He has also installed every proprietary profitability software application on the market for other clients.

He is a recognized speaker and writer in the field of cost accounting and profitability analysis.

He has forty plus years of cost accounting and profitability analysis experience in the manufacturing, retail and financial industries. This includes the development of unique work measurement Systems for the financial industry.

Check out his videos on YouTube.

Thomas N. Gerry

Tom Gerry has 40 years experience as a proven team leader, salesperson, consultant, entrepreneur, speaker and author. He has broad experience in marketing, sales, implementations and training. Tom managed application development projects of shrink wrapped and semi-custom financial institution software.

Tom has been a client and has collaborated on consulting engagements with Resource Management Associates for over 25 years.

Tom founded three consulting businesses and a technology company-one reached $20 million in sales. He led the creation of a performance advisory services group to enhance technology ROI and improve processes at banks and credit unions. He has published a book on payments innovations being applied for profit improvement and competitive advantage in businesses, non profits, and community financial institutions.

He has leadership skills in setting strategic direction and creating winning competitive campaigns – one company achieved #1 national ranking in branch automation. He has helped early stage companies build business plans, projection models and private placement offerings resulting in multiple rounds of venture investment.

Tom has excellent communication skills – he has authored white papers, been quoted in industry publications, created and delivered seminars and a webinar series, and made speeches at national and regional conventions.

Besides leadership roles at several startup companies, and starting a business unit of Harland Clarke, Tom worked with Kirchman, Systeme Corporation, Citicorp Information Resources, Financial Data Systems, Boeing Computer Services, and Citizens & Southern Bank in Atlanta.

Tom is an honors graduate of the University of Florida with a BSBA in Finance and Banking.

Learn about the value his book and his approach are uncovering at www.PaymentsPower.com. Check out his videos on YouTube.

Resource Management Associates

Resource Management Associates (RMA) is a consulting firm founded in 1980 to serve financial institutions. Our clients include commercial banks, savings banks, credit unions and mortgage banks throughout the United States. RMA delivers unique professional services blending the disciplines of industrial engineering into performance improvement through cost accounting, project management, and technology and payments vendor management.

RMA's consulting approach is "hands on." We identify needs, train people, design the solution, plan and oversee the implementation. Our deliverables have been developed in the field, not in an office or academic environment.

Over the past thirty plus years we have created, and continually improved practical solutions to difficult challenges in the financial industry. The initial assignment for our first client in early 1981 was a cost accounting and organizational profitability project. Since then the system has been refined and advanced to Simplified Profitability, the subject of this book.

Edward B. Ginn, PE is President of RMA and is the primary author. Tom Gerry serves as a Vice President of RMA, and has contributed content, editing, design and publishing through knAct, LLC.

RMA Strengths

In addition to Simplified Profitability for organization responsibility centers, we also extend this foundation for our clients to perform product and customer cost accounting and profitability analysis. Those are the subjects of two future volumes we will publish.

Our deep experience in technology system evaluation and selection has led to our proprietary migration studies that compare the total cost over a six to ten year period of the strategic alternatives of in-house vs. outsourced core, items and ATM/Debit processing with the associated disaster recovery.

We are noted for our business continuity approach that adds the practical planning and testing for the financial institutions' people as well as the infrastructure.

We have applied the unique RMA cost accounting, evaluation and selection techniques with the comprehensive payments approach described in the book, *Payments Power,* authored by Tom Gerry, to create performance improvement programs for ATM/Debit processing, and a unique merchant services competitive strategy.

Part 1

Set the Stage

To create or construct a Simplified Profitability system requires understanding of concepts, terms and techniques that have primarily been developed and refined in manufacturing and industry.

Part 1 establishes a foundation based on this knowledge set adapted to financial institutions. Then in Part 2 you will find the initial management decisions that add building blocks on the foundation, the stage set in this part.

There are four chapters in Part 1, which include nine workplan steps:

Chapter 1 introduces an overview which explains quickly the elements of the RMA system that ensures simplicity.

Chapter 2 explains the essential concepts and steps that must be executed to enable on-going data generation. In addition, the financial institution team members are chosen and educated.

Chapter 3 illustrates how simple activity based drivers are identified and used for charging service center costs to profit centers. The techniques for charging shared space to various service and profit centers are illustrated with examples.

Chapter 4 adds more foundation building blocks with definitions and lays out the work necessary for the team to present the initial options and recommendations for management decisions in Part 2.

Activity Based

www.SimplifiedProfitability.com

Chapter 1

System Overview

This chapter reviews the purpose of organization cost accounting & profitability analysis. We review the strength and simplicity of the RMA actual cost approach.

We set the foundation with a quick definition of the three types of responsibility centers:

1. Profit
2. Service
3. General Overhead

Before banking, my experience included being responsible for the labor and material standards in several manufacturing companies. In the mid-70s, when my career path shifted to banking, I received a real culture shock. Bankers were offended when asked about products. They believed they only offered services and could not define anything that resembled a product. Overhead seemed to cover everything. Work measurement was for efficiency experts. Finally, when I realized that money was the inventory, a new creative career began.

This book is written in order to answer two basic questions:

- What is the actual contribution to profit by each organization (business unit)?
- What are the specific profit improvement opportunities within each organization?

This book is directed primarily to financial institutions.

Those that would be interested in this book would be responsible officers interested in identifying the contribution to the bottom line by the organizations within the bank. They would then take action based on this information. This is usually the CEO, COO or CFO but not limited to this level. It will often depend on the size and the culture of the institution.

The book's objective is to describe the steps necessary to develop and implement an Organization Profitability Reporting & Analysis system that is an activity based cost accounting system. The system will have full absorption and an easily understood charge out of service centers like loan operations and core processing; it will also have an easily understood funds transfer method. The system will balance to the bank's general ledger in a logical and practical way.

In addition the book will provide the following solutions:

- Sound and practical cost accounting methods that can consistently measure organization profitability.
- A participative approach to implementation so that everyone understands and assumes ownership.
- A timely approach to implementation so that by the time the system is developed everyone has not forgotten the purpose or lost interest. Three to four months is a good time frame.

The book concentrates on the bank staff and management receiving their training in cost accounting concepts and understanding the process. This can be accomplished using the bank's existing general ledger and core processing applications supplemented by report writers and spreadsheet processing, or it can be accomplished using the latest techniques of automation. There are some great software systems out there.

The greatest software system is useless if the concepts are not clearly understood.

This book does not address the choice of whether it will be fully automated, integrated spreadsheet processing, or even manual. It addresses understanding the concepts in a practical manner.

There should be a few words about the executives and their involvement in the decision to design and implement a cost accounting and profitability system. Later we will discuss in detail the characteristics and the selection of the analyst or the staff people who will actually do the work.

The greatest success in cost accounting and profitability systems has been with the executives that have some experience with a manufacturing or retail cost accounting system. This can be through hands-on line management or auditing experience.

At the opposite end of the spectrum are those executives that have learned something one way and one way only, and refused to believe there's a better way to accomplish the desired result.

In between are a lot of great people who have argued, but maintained an open mind in relation to achieving a profitability measurement system that can result in action plans for improvement. This requires a combination of accounting and work measurement knowledge. Adding to this is the ability to develop mathematical models to express the results which produces a very desirable outcome.

Understanding cost accounting concepts is much more important than the calculations. You can perform thousands of complex calculations, but if you are calculating the wrong thing, there is a problem. If you are performing many, many calculations thinking the detail is accuracy instead of using sound work measurement principles, the results will be poor at best, or will lead to wrong conclusions, at worst.

PURPOSE OF ORGANIZATION COST ACCOUNTING & PROFITABILITY ANALYSIS

Profitability Reporting measures profitability of the bank as a whole and its component organizations. This would include but not be limited to branches, lending and trust department. This is usually performed during a specified period, monthly or quarterly. It reflects all past decisions whether good or bad and their effect in the period of measurement. Examples are rates paid, rates charged, charge-offs, losses, liquidity, credit decisions, inflation, deflation, labor relations, regulatory relations, the economy, etc., etc. Profitability Reporting must always balance to the bank's General Ledger within reason, usually 1%.

The purpose of Profitability Reporting is to analyze the contribution of each individual profit center to the total profit of the Bank. This means a fully burdened cost system which accounts for 100% of all income and expense. It presents the actual income & expense in a standard cost "format" that recovers a fair share of overhead from all units. It should present as accurate as possible reports that can be understood by the unit managers. Activity based charge out methods based on sound work measurement techniques avoid the problems of "negotiated' costs. Simplicity and understandability is the key to success. Success is defined as control of profitability of the bank through improvement strategies of the components.

If control of profitability is the objective, the key to success is variance analysis. This means asking the question WHY? Not only why something is not good, but why something is producing great results.

Many times management wants to complicate the measurement system by introducing components that produce no significant profit improvement strategy. An example of this type of complication is the argument of single pool of funds vs. the multiple pools of funds. It is simpler to begin with a single pool of funds.

Improvement strategies will fall into one of the following areas:

1. Financial: Sale, sale & leaseback of branch or office facilities
2. Marketing/Pricing: Increase balances, proper rate mix, rate/volume analysis
3. Operational: Productivity improvements

A profitability reporting system reports "what it is" during a specified period. Analysis answers the question WHY. Do not complicate or confuse the profitability reporting tool with other analytical tools. Performance analysis is made up of many tools.

Before you even start reading the book, here is a useful overview framework. You will find that some reference books may use synonymous terms. Careful examination will reveal that they are one and the same.

The purpose of this cost accounting & profitability reporting system is to report (measure, analyze, determine) the actual cost of an organization (profit center) within a financial institution. It will be reported in a standard cost format (three tiers) which recovers a fair share of overhead from all units. Please see the diagram on the next page.

A strong premise of the system is to determine the actual cost and profitability rather than what it should cost. Determining the actual cost is the first step of determining what it should cost!! This approach is often referred to as a fully burdened basis for each profit center. This means the profit centers absorb all expenses and include all income.

The goal of the cost accounting system is to charge out expense directly to the using responsibility center as opposed to accumulating and reallocating in an excessively complex procedure. This allows end users to understand appropriate charges to their responsibility centers. Responsibility center closeouts will not exceed two levels.

The system will use activity based cost accounting techniques to charge out expenses to using responsibility centers. Activities will be selected such as accounts opened, loans closed, accounts on record, transactions, etc. Arbitrary percentages or negotiated cost will not occur.

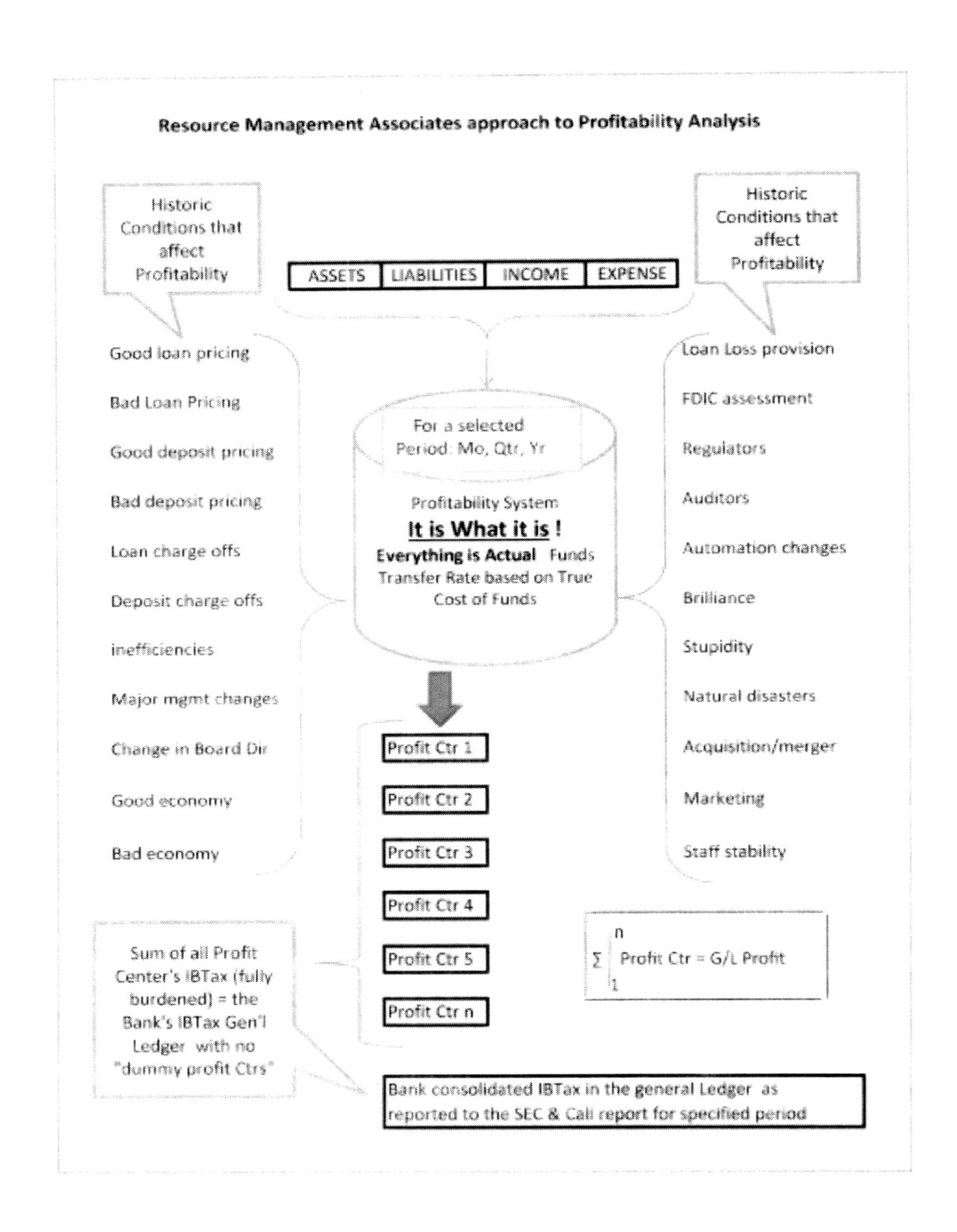
Resource Management Associates approach to Profitability Analysis
Historic Conditions that affect Profitability
ASSETS
LIABILITIES
INCOME
EXPENSE
Historic Conditions that affect Profitability
Good loan pricing
Bad Loan Pricing
Good deposit pricing
Bad deposit pricing
Loan charge offs
Deposit charge offs
inefficiencies
Major mgmt changes
Change in Board Dir
Good economy
Bad economy
For a selected Period: Mo, Qtr, Yr
Profitability System
It is What it is !
Everything is Actual Funds Transfer Rate based on True Cost of Funds
Loan Loss provision
FDIC assessment
Regulators
Auditors
Automation changes
Brilliance
Stupidity
Natural disasters
Acquisition/merger
Marketing
Staff stability
Profit Ctr 1
Profit Ctr 2
Profit Ctr 3
Profit Ctr 4
Profit Ctr 5
Profit Ctr n
Sum of all Profit Center's IBTax (fully burdened) = the Bank's IBTax Gen'l Ledger with no "dummy profit Ctrs"
Σ n 1 Profit Ctr = G/L Profit
Bank consolidated IBTax in the general Ledger as reported to the SEC & Call report for specified period

ORGANIZATION DEFINITION AND HIERARCHY

Responsibility Center: An organizational unit performing duties with a common goal so as to fulfill a responsibility of the organization. A responsibility center is further classified as follows:

- Profit Center: A responsibility center which generates income by selling a product(s) or performing a service, thus creating a profit. For example, a branch, trust department, investment department, or a commercial loan department.
- Service Center: A responsibility center whose duty is to provide service in the operation of profit centers. The costs a service center incurs are charged to all responsibility centers it services based on activity drivers. For example, core data processing, deposit operations, bookkeeping, ATM/Debit processing or Electronic Banking.
- General Overhead Center: A responsibility center whose duty results just from being in business. For example, executive management, human resources, accounting or directors' expenses.

Activity Based

www.SimplifiedProfitability.com

CHAPTER 2

FOUNDATION BUILDING BLOCKS

In this chapter we explore and illustrate several key cost accounting concepts essential for building the Simplified Profitability models.

Then we focus on the teamwork for success. The selection of project participants, analysts, is described.

Several case studies help explain how to determine responsibility centers in the accounting systems.

To document processes, we present instructions and examples of a simple, but powerful industrial engineering tool adapted for financial institutions - THE WORK DISTRIBUTION CHART.

COST ACCOUNTING CONCEPTS

Whether manual, spreadsheet, a spreadsheet augmented by some download (Cognos), or fully automated software system, the following must be understood:

- Sequential Closeouts
- Conceptual Flow
- Level of Detail & Accuracy
- Data Base (Set Up Files)

This chapter offers various graphics for discussion. It is sort of an appendix only early in the documentation.

Closeouts

There are several places in this book that will refer to "closeouts". It is necessary to create a definition of what the word closeout means so that the diagrams in the book will be more useful.

If you look on the Internet and look up the definition of closeout you might run into the definition from the retail business. It defines it as a sale on all goods in liquidating a business. Liquidation is a term used frequently in business when it is closing its doors.

In cost accounting a closeout is the act of charging out (liquidating) all cost within a responsibility center (or cost center) and recording (adding) them in a another appropriate responsibility center(s). One center can charge out to one or more centers. These are sequential closeouts.

An objective of Simplified Profitability is to minimize the number of sequential closeouts within a system. We typically never have more than two closeouts. Otherwise, the results become vague and hard to understand.

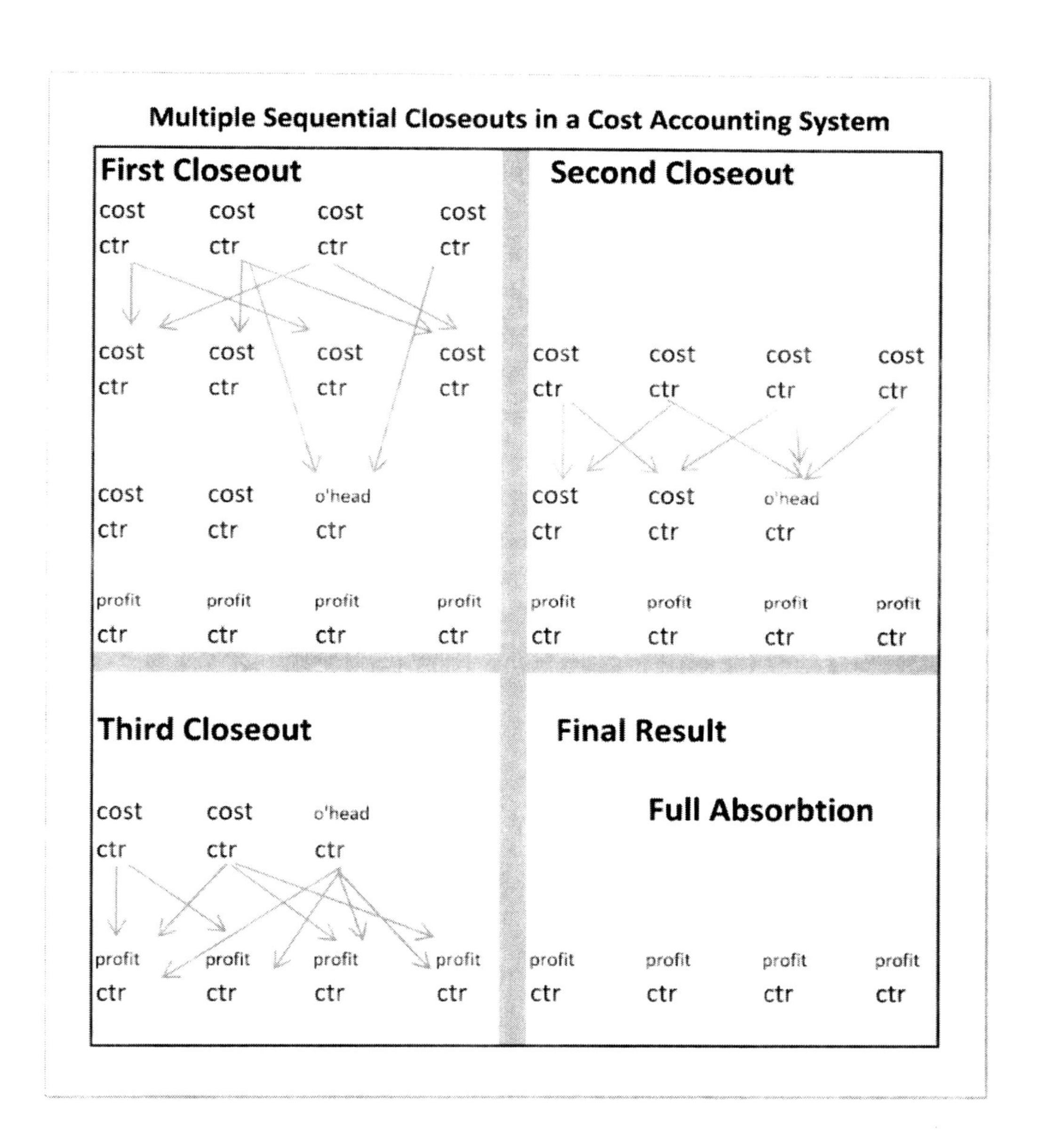

This diagram seems complicated. More than two closeout steps confuses people - one of the common obstacles to acceptance of cost accounting results. Simplified Profitability minimizes the number of closeouts to just two as shown on the next page.

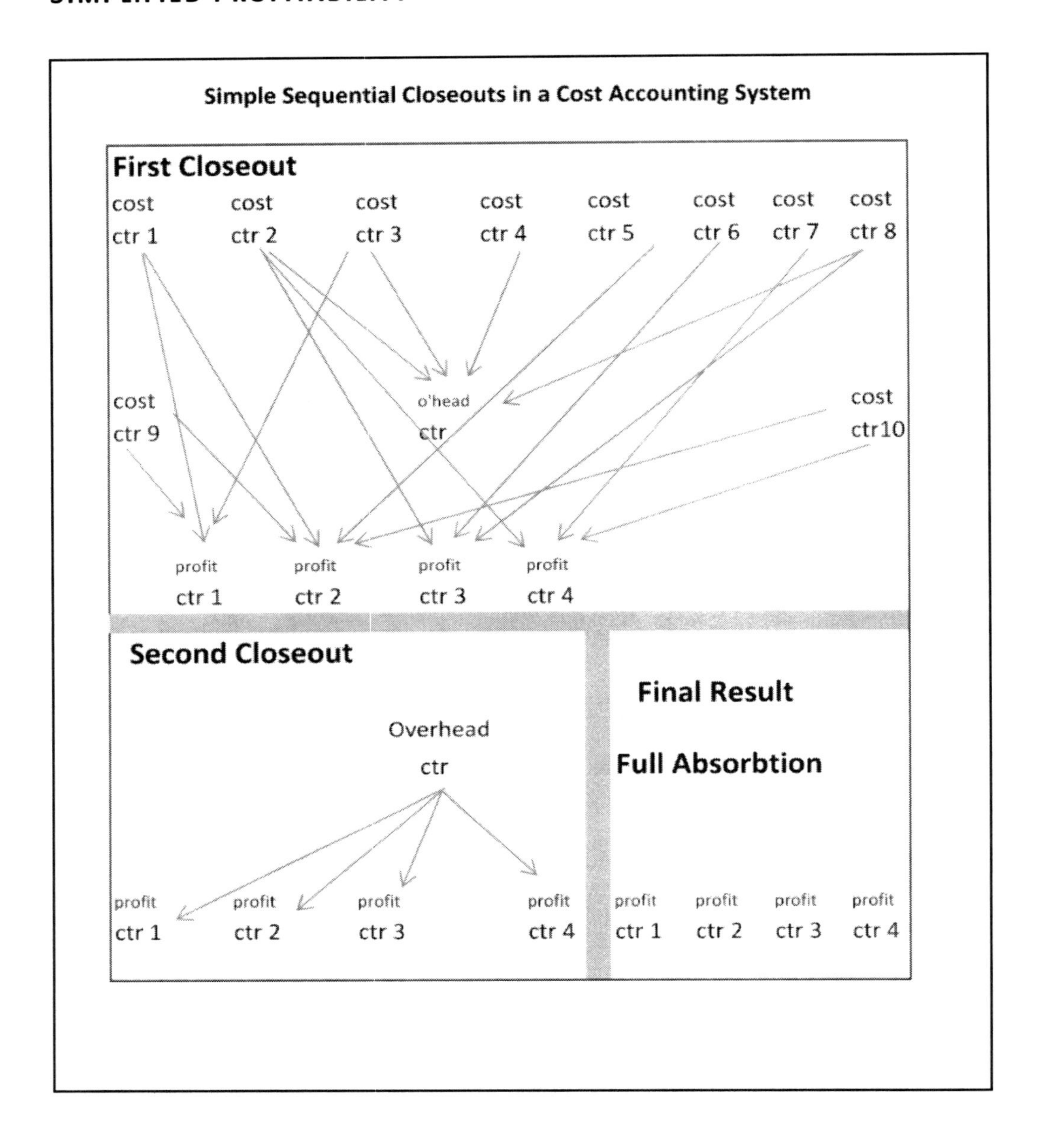

The first closeout step assigns costs to all responsibility centers, including overhead, with activity drivers to profit centers.

The second closeout then allocates the overhead to profit centers.

These two simple to understand steps are one of the secrets to the effectiveness and acceptance of the Simplified Profitability approach. This should be clear to people that do not have an accounting background.

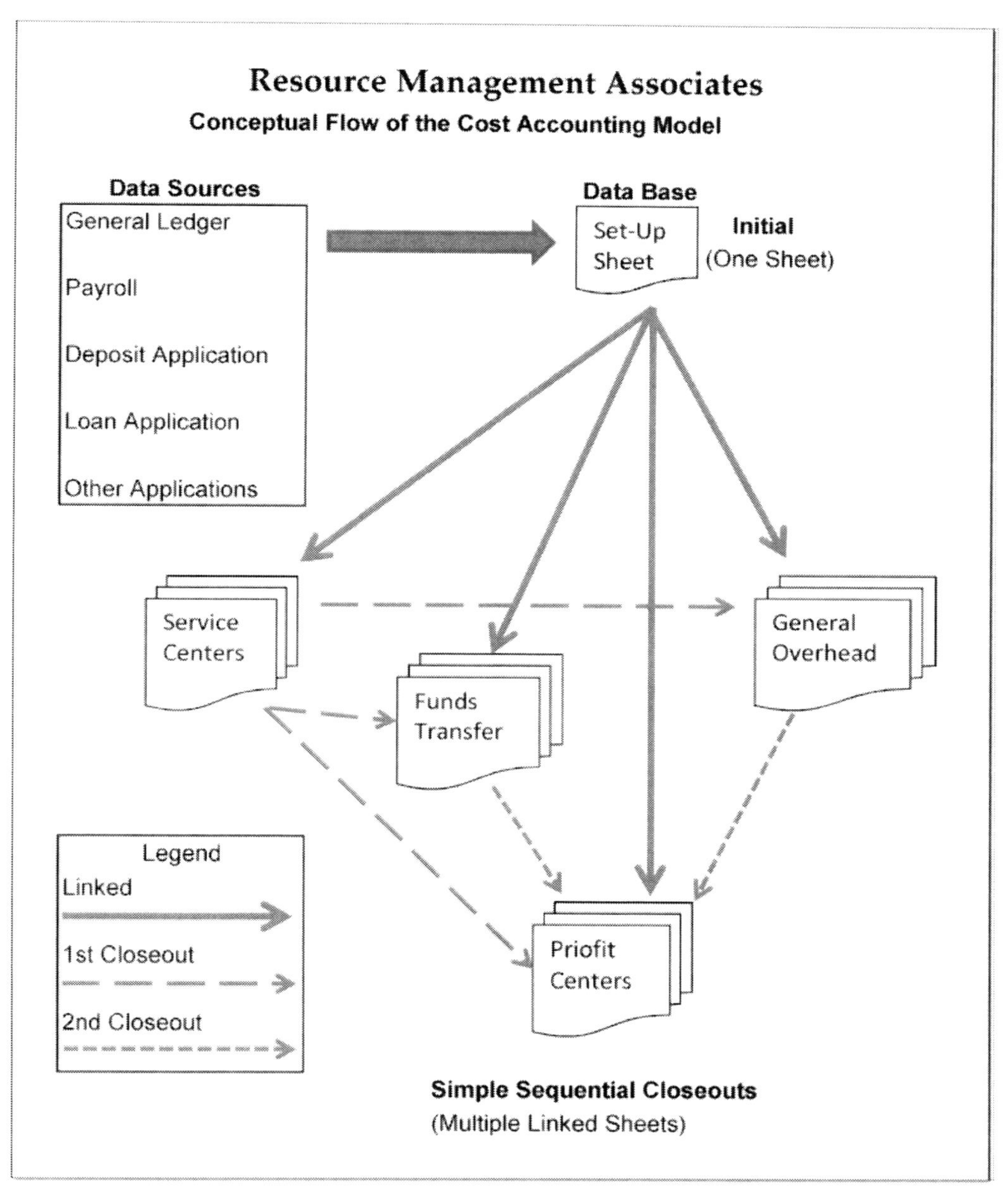

In the above diagram the various data sources feed the database. This can be a worksheet in a spreadsheet file or an internal data base in a sophisticated software system.

This accumulates and distributes the data (or is linked) to the appropriate responsibility centers. Through algorithms, the first closeout occurs and then the second closeout occurs to produce the final result - also quite accurate as shown next.

Bank Name | **Organization Cost & Profitability Analysis**

Period | 3rd Qtr 2000

	Branch Name			
Total Deposits	$ 32,449,156			
Available Capital	$ 1,462,366			
Total Gross Loans	$ 2,376,967		Expected	Effective
		Per Cent	Per Cent	Per cent
		of Total	Accurate	Accurate
Income		D	E	=D * E
Fees, Misc	$ 46,007	7.2%	85%	6.12%
Interest	$ 57,109	8.9%	100%	8.94%
Funds earning credit	$ 535,805	83.9%	100%	83.86%
Total	$ 638,921	100.0%		98.92% Accuracy
Expenses				
Direct & Indirect				
Salaries & Benefits	$ 74,734	14.4%	99%	14.24%
All Other	$ 38,448	7.4%	85%	6.29%
Service center charges				
Data Processing	$ 23,613	4.5%	95%	4.32%
Deposit Processing	$ 25,919	5.0%	95%	4.74%
Items Processing	$ 5,575	1.1%	95%	1.02%
Loan Operations	$ 1,214	0.2%	95%	0.22%
Network	$ 1,036	0.2%	95%	0.19%
Branch Indirect	$ 3,883	0.7%	95%	0.71%
Loan Indirect	$ 1,768	0.3%	95%	0.32%
Interest Expense	$ 241,249	46.4%	100%	46.44%
General Overhead	$ 64,534	12.4%	95%	11.80%
Funds use charge	$ 37,556	7.2%	100%	7.23%
Total	$ 519,529	100.0%		97.52% Accuracy
Net Profit	$ 119,392			

ACCURACY ANALYSIS : ACTUAL ORGANIZATIONAL PROFITABILITY

This shows the weighted impact of accuracy by line item. It then shows the aggregate total impact for both Income and Expense. An example would be that a line item that is only 90% accurate and makes up less than 10% of the total (100%) has far less impact than a line item that is 100% accurate and makes up more than 50% of the total (100%)

Set-Up Sheet Period 2nd QTR **Cost accounting Data Base**

Example Natl Bank

Responsibility Cnt		Balances		Income		
		Deposits	Loans & Inv	Deposit Fees	Loan Fees	Interest Income
Branch	1	214,392,486	175,305,498	172,146	231,674	2,356,351
Branch	2	46,517,339	42,970,364	63,184	23,566	655,942
Branch	3	9,782,934	1,241,611	27,825	2,247	21,416
Branch	4	25,991,942	3,087,647	37,936	3,072	51,748
Branch	5	5,768,047	17,394	15,343	509	294
Branch	6	45,905,515	26,535,797	57,597	34,151	370,291
Branch	7	13,230,127	3,992,885	18,041	1,888	64,962
Branch	8	6,814,642	1,457,214	9,682	1,010	24,667
Branch	9	60,053,412	35,240,034	79,041	21,467	504,956
Invest PC	51		165,535,061			1,576,226
Trust PC	55			236,811		
Loan PC	57					
Loan Ops	60					
Deposit Ops	61			160,575		
Branch Admin	62					
Network	63					
Item Process	64					
Data Process	65					
Ops Admin	66					
HR/Mkt	70					
Accounting	71					
Executive	72					
GOH Admin	73					
Treasury	74					
M Office Ind	75					
TOTALS		428,456,444	289,848,445	878,180	319,582	4,050,626
			165,535,061			1,576,226
			455,383,506			5,626,852
Amount to spread						
Capital		54,520,346				
Non earning assets		27,958,969				

Here is an example of the balances and income responsibility center database for a quarterly period. This can be input to a spreadsheet as shown here, or interfaced from source systems into an automated profitability application.

Set-Up Sheet Period 2nd QTR **Cost accounting Data Base**

Example Natl Bank

	Resp Cntr	Expense						
		Interest Expense	Salaries	Benefits	Direct Expense	Indirect Expense	FDIC Ins	Prov for Ln Loss
Branch	1	866,511	192,214	87,526	113,931		91,272	208,662
Branch	2	164,502	81,053	36,908	47,712		19,804	51,147
Branch	3	30,307	18,098	8,241	12,732		4,165	1,478
Branch	4	92,229	29,617	13,486	30,253		11,065	3,675
Branch	5	18,037	19,734	8,986	11,175		2,456	21
Branch	6	201,738	77,364	35,228	21,747		19,543	31,585
Branch	7	49,009	15,692	7,145	8,694		5,632	4,753
Branch	8	26,170	13,387	6,096	11,116		2,901	1,734
Branch	9	209,898	89,351	40,687	60,525		25,566	41,945
Invest	51		0	0	305			
Trust	55		78,798	35,881	34,122			
Loan	57		0	0	0			
Ln Ops	60		98,412	44,812	24,918			
Dep Ops	61		38,905	17,716	91,409			
Br Adm	62		32,047	14,593	0			
Network	63		11,390	5,186	83,739			
Item Pro	64		13,804	6,286	2,927			
Data Pro	65		11,058	5,035	115,898			
Ops Adm	66		25,572	11,644	965			
HR/Mkt	70		35,464	16,149	28,953			
Acctg	71		66,644	30,347	2,655			
Exec	72		0	0	0	17,700		
G o'head	73		115,731	52,699	218,499			
Treasury	74		0	0	0			
M O Ind	75			0	33,168			
TOTALS		1,658,400	1,064,335	484,654	955,439	17,700	182,404	345,000
Amount to spread				484,654			182,404	345,000

And here are the interest and non interest expenses.

Note that the FDIC assessment and the provision for loan losses are recorded in separate fields so they can be reported separately in the profit center performance reports.

The following page shows examples of statistical drivers chosen for the activity based cost chargeouts, and other purposes.

Set-Up Sheet Period: 2nd QTR — **Cost accounting Data Base**

	Resp Center	Deposit # accounts	Loan # accounts	Number Wkstation
		Statistics		
Branch	1	11221	3911	22
Branch	2	3264	1689	15
Branch	3	1200	100	6
Branch	4	2675	261	9
Branch	5	841	0	6
Branch	6	3803	1144	13
Branch	7	1296	204	5
Branch	8	784	85	6
Branch	9	4765	1529	18
Investment PC	51			
Trust PC	55			8
Loan PC	57			
Loan Operations	60			11
Deposit Operations	61			8
Branch Administration	62			
Network	63			1
Item Processing	64			6
Data Processing (Core)	65			1
Operations Administration	66			2
HR/Marketing	70			2
Accounting	71			5
Executive	72			
GOH Administration	73			5
Treasury	74			
Main Office Indirect	75			
TOTALS		29849	8923	149

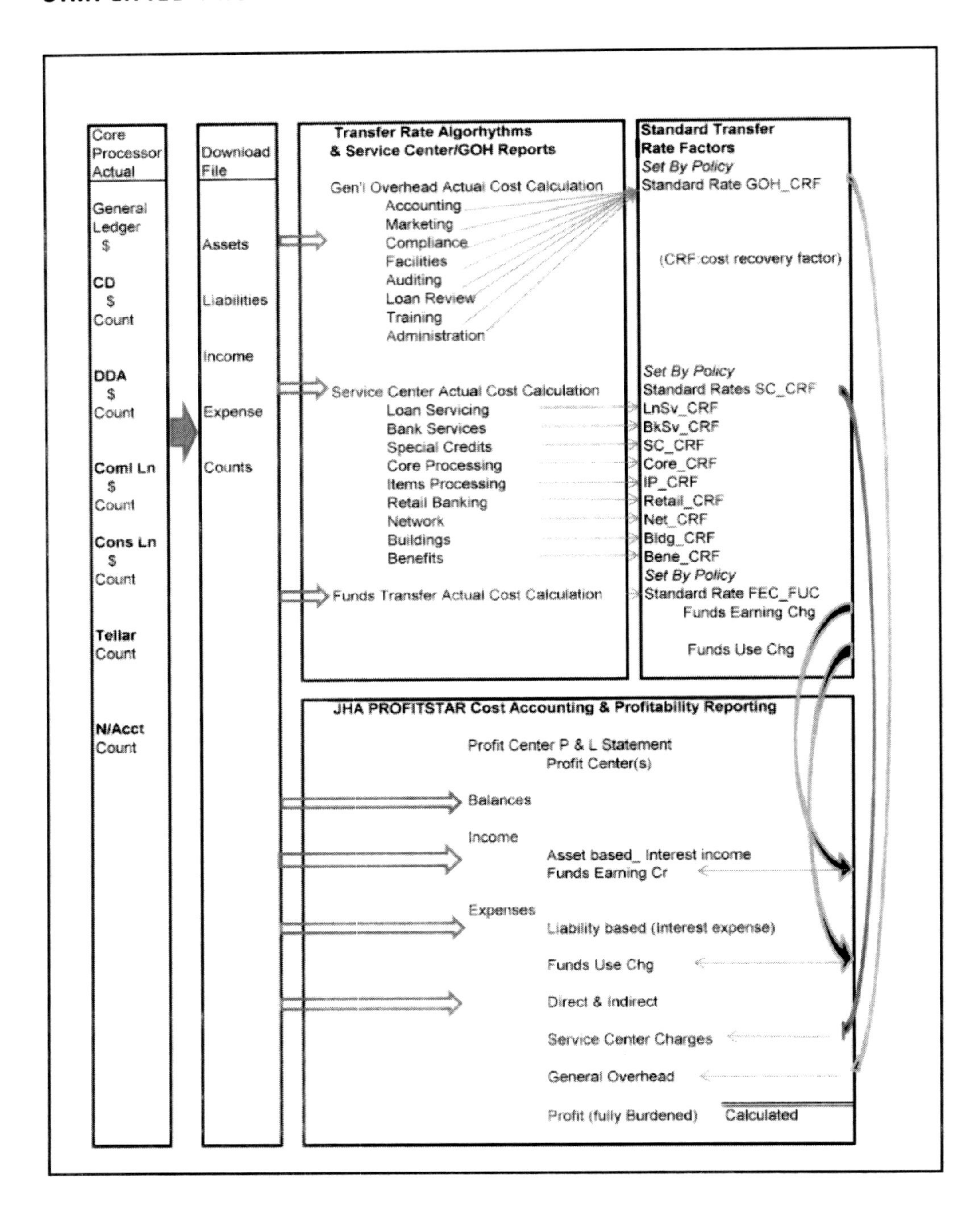

This diagram is an example of the flow of information within a cost accounting software application (in contrast to the previous pages of spreadsheet examples).

SELECT ANALYSTS

The approach that has been most successful is to make the development of the project involve more than just accounting personnel. In many cases one or more analysts are named to gather the information and develop the system. This adds immeasurably to the acceptance of the system once it's introduced.

This typically identifies a person or persons who can do all of the detail research, follow the work plan developed with senior management's approval and organize the appropriate intermediate and final presentation. This is usually someone from accounting or operations who has access to many data sources. However, analysts have come from many ranks, i.e., audit, operations, etc. The analysts must be able to spend approximately 25 – 35% of their time on the project if it is to be completed in 3 to 4 months.

Select a ***good analyst***.

Selection of an analyst should have nothing to do with age or gender. A good analyst has a strong work ethic, intelligence, curiosity, and is typically accepted by peers or generally known as a 'People' person. All of these are very good characteristics of an analyst that you want on a team. Keep in mind that this person must be able to follow instructions and work with employees to get the data.

Another challenge in selecting the analyst is sometimes their manager is reluctant to assign someone because they feel that the analyst is going to make decisions. The analyst actually does the legwork or the detail work to develop alternatives; supervisors and managers make the decision as to how things will be done.

Quite often when management starts saying "we can't spare that person", that is really the person you need because they are the doers and get things done. In most assignments the analyst is not dedicated 100%, but is more likely required to apply 25% of their time to the project. This leads to the management challenge - they must find alternative resources to do that 25%. For example, an analyst's 40 hour week goes to a 50 hour week and that's exactly what you do not want to happen. It becomes a balancing act to get the supervisors to allow the analyst time in order to do the work for the project.

Case History: Examples of unusual analysts that have been exceptionally successful.

- A grandmother, who had raised her family, returned to school and then re-entered the work force.
- A women who had worked as teller, new accounts, check processing, bookkeeping and accounting and was found in the auditing department.
- A women who was buried in the back room running and maintaining a reader sorter, and managing a very efficient shop. Her IQ was ***off the charts***. She had never been given a chance to advance further. (She was 20 years younger than the others in the department).
- A lady who was very experienced in all areas of operations and worked in a bank with an ethnic group that was primarily matriarchal in their family matters.
- A bright teller who had indicated a desire to ***climb the ladder*** and do more.
- A bright young man who had entered an accounting department from another industry. He was eager to learn banking processes and he didn't have to ***unlearn*** anything.
- A person from the training department who was a great trainer, but needed to learn more about the processes and jobs that she was training.

Case History: The motivated analyst.

You must not only select good analysts, you must train and motivate them. In the case of an organization cost accounting project we typically teach the analysts how to gather the information and document it in the form of a work distribution chart. We also teach interview techniques to get the right information.

Motivation comes in the form of getting the analyst the right tools and techniques, encouraging them, and enabling them. Sometimes enabling merely means giving them the time to do the analyst work in addition to their normal work.

There was the case of three analysts being trained and at the end of the first day they were given the assignment to come to work the next morning by a different route. This, of course, was to get them to think differently and to try something new. One of the analysts came in to the session the next morning 30 minutes later than normal. His explanation was his new route was terrible. The point was made. He was able to try an alternative that did not work well, but it was only affecting him. He was not making a mistake with a group of people or with resources of the bank. Care should be taken not to overly motivate analysts. They will surprise you.

DETERMINE RESPONSIBILITY CENTERS

When general ledger is developed and set up in a bank, ideally there will be departments or responsibility centers set up in order to classify income and expenses in the department responsible for them, i.e. charging a branch for its electricity, charging loan servicing for their office supplies, etc. Responsibility centers are then further classified into profit center, service center or general overhead. This requires a review of the general ledger departmentalization and the Bank's organization chart, if available.

Each unique organizational unit will correspond to the Bank's organization chart. Each item on an organization chart should be identified in the general ledger as a responsibility center. If the units from the chart cannot be identified in the general ledger, add the appropriate responsibility centers (departments) to general ledger. Next, each responsibility center is classified as being a profit center, a service center or a general overhead center.

The general overhead centers will range in count from three to nine and include accounting, executive and human resources.

Service centers will range in count from five to nine and include data processing, item processing and branch administration.

Profit centers are net income producing centers and will include all branches (including Main Office) plus three to five other profit centers such as investments or trust.

There is no exact template to cover the design of how many responsibility centers are required. A well designed general ledger will serve as a database for sound account reporting and control, regulatory reporting, budgeting, performance reporting and finally cost accounting and profitability reporting.

A bank with forty plus branches will require a general ledger that can handle a three digit responsibility number. Asset size has nothing to do with this design criteria. There are banks that have only five branches that exceed five million in assets.

Case History: Defining unused facilities as profit centers.

This is the story of facilities planning and how bank owned properties that are not other real estate owned can be approached. This particular bank had developed new buildings and had a great deal of idle facilities that would impact existing profit centers should they have to pay or absorb the cost of unproductive square footage. Moreover, they were in no way being controlled. Each with unused space became a responsibility center. The center was losing money but at least it was identified and managed.

As an example there was a building with three levels. The main level was the retail branch. The lower level was the accounting department, which was part of the general overhead. The second level was the executive offices which were now vacant because of a new headquarters building. By identifying the three levels as separate facilities, the branch would not have to absorb the under utilized space of the second level. It also provided a cost base for rental purposes.

Case History: Defining "Special Assets" as a profit center.

A community bank was making the transition from a real estate based lending bank to commercial and industrial accounts. This included moving from CD based funding to demand deposit funding. This is not an easy task.

Confusing the issue was the problem of dealing with the non-accruing and ORE assets, Other Real Estate Owned, that required attention. A useful solution was selected that placed all assets, income, and expense in a responsibility center. The cost and effort to maintain and dispose was then highlighted and better managed. The other profit centers were not encumbered with carrying that burden. In addition, progress in reducing this profit drain was clearly in focus for senior management, directors and regulators.

Case History: The case of aligning costs with income.

This is a story of the lady who managed the ATM Department. She wanted to be known as a profit center. She felt that since she received the fees for foreign transactions that she should be a profit center. However, when the explanation came that she would also incur the expense of the ATM driver or computers support, the branch person that serviced the ATM, the depreciation of the ATM, staff, and the outside vendor servicing of the ATM, she decided that she would probably be better off being a service center as opposed to a profit center. Many departments that receive certain fees do not realize that if they are to be a profit center they must also incur the cost associated with generating that fee income.

Case History: Where do consumer loans belong? Centralized or decentralized.

Commercial loans are typically originated and serviced centrally. Consumer loans can be serviced centrally but originated in the branch system. There are two possibilities. The consumer loans can be originated in the branch and serviced centrally. In this case the branch is the profit center and receives a charge for servicing the loans originated in that branch based on the number of loans serviced. An alternative way is to originate loans in the branch and book them centrally and let the central profit center receive a charge for the origination process. In either event, it is a question of aligning the interest and fee income with the cost to originate and service that asset.

Case History: Defining administration service centers to summarize confidential salaries.

The fact is that salaries of officers and employees are and should be confidential. Experience shows that one of the restraints on organizational profitability analysis is the reluctance of bankers to reveal even groupings of salary totals. Some banks border on paranoia.

With that in mind it is very clear that salary groupings for profitability analysis should never be less than three employees. Isolating one employee is not smart. Reporting two is not good because if I know what I make I can figure out the other person's rate. It is always wise to group officers and employees together for this purpose. Avoid revealing a single person's salary.

A clever device that one bank used when they found some branches had only one officer was to create a branch administration service center to accumulate branch management salaries which was then charged out to each branch on an equitable basis. This also works in smaller banks for general overhead salaries.

An example of a bank's general ledger/responsibility center design			
Description	**RC#**	**Classification**	
Bank Roll-up	99	Bank	
Other Roll-ups	90-98	Bank	
Future growth	75-79	GOH	Admin Centers are designed to accumulate salary & related accounts where confidentiality may be an issue
Treasury	74	GOH	
Administration	73	GOH	
Executive	72	GOH	
Accounting	71	GOH	
HR/Marketing	70	GOH	
Expansion	67-69	Service Center	Service centers occur in every bank no matter what size. They require sequential closeout to the responsibility centers that use them.
Operations Admin	66	Service Center	
Data Processing Core	65	Service Center	
Item Processing	64	Service Center	
Network	63	Service Center	
Branch Admin	62	Service Center	
Deposit Operations	61	Service Center	
Loan Operations	60	Service Center	

Example Bank
Profitability Project
Responsibility Center Classifications

Profit center	PC
Service center	SC
General overhead	GOH

Resp Ctr #	Description	
1	Burlington Branch	PC
2	Langley Branch	PC
4	Oak Harbor Branch	PC
5	Coupeville Branch	PC
6	Clinton Branch	PC
7	Camano Island Branch	PC
8	Midway Branch	PC
10	Bellingham Branch	PC
12	Freeland Branch	PC
14	Anacortes Branch	PC
16	Dealer/Consumer Loan Center	PC
17	Sedro Woolley Branch	PC
18	College Way Branch	PC
19	Bakerview Branch	PC
20	Stanwood Branch	PC
21	Fairhaven Branch	PC
22	Smokey Point Branch	PC
25	Northwest Branch	PC
26	Friday Harbor Branch	PC
50	Burlington Financial Center	SC
51	Oak Harbor Financial Center	SC
52	Oak Harbor Admin - Bayshore	SC
53	New Burlington Admin Center	SC
54	New Bulding Profit Center	PC
56	Commercial Division (new)	PC
58	Real Estate Lending	PC
64	Investment Products	PC
69	Network (Currently Info Tech)	SC
70	Accounting	GOH
71	Loan Servicing	SC
72	Marketing	GOH
73	Compliance	GOH
74	Facilities	GOH
75	Bank Services	SC
78	Loan Administration/Special Credits	SC
79	Core Processing (Currently Info Systems)	SC
80	Auditing	GOH
82	Loan Review	SC
83	Private Banking	PC
84	Human Resources	GOH
85	Item Processing	SC
86	Retail Banking	SC
88	SBA Department	PC
89	Training	GOH
92	Bank Investments (new)	PC
93	Administration	GOH
99	Consolidated	

Expansion	58-59	Profit Center	These are true Profit centers. They represent a variable number of centers and could be unprofitable initially.
Loans	57	Profit Center	
Trust	55	Profit Center	
Investments	51	Profit Center	
Main Office Branch	01	Profit Center	
Branch	02	Profit Center	
Branch	03	Profit Center	
Branch	04	Profit Center	
Branch	05	Profit Center	
Branch	06	Profit Center	
Branch	07	Profit Center	
Branch	08	Profit Center	
Branch	09	Profit Center	
Expansion	10-40	Profit Center	

DOCUMENT APPROPRIATE PROCESSES

A Work Distribution Chart is an excellent tool to measure and document departments (service centers) that perform support functions to multiple profit centers. Examples are a deposit operations service center that performs some functions for the loan profit center, or a branch that performs both deposit and loan functions. Measure a typical week or month.

Case History: Splitting Service Center charges to multiple Profit Centers

This is about a service center underwriting and processing for both the indirect loan office and all of the branches. A work distribution chart showed clearly that processing and underwriting for the branches required 40% of the service center time, and the indirect loans used 60%.

In a senior management meeting when these decisions were being reviewed, the senior officer for branches immediately became defensive, saying that branches should not be charged for 40% of the service centers' cost. But, when he looked closely at the chart shown on the next page, he could clearly see, that based on the supervisor's estimate, that it would be 40% to process for the branches. When process documentation is properly used, these types of arguments disappear.

Work Distribution Chart		Dealer Center					Date	6/29/2009		
Function: Branch Underwriting		**Hours in .5 hour increments per week**								
Tasks	% of time	Total Hours	Mgr	Cons Ln II	Cons Ln I	Cons Ln II	Cr Asst	Cr Asst	Ln Per	Ln Per
Processing & doc prep - consumer & RE	35%	45.5	2.5	6	6	6	13	12.5		
Pull Apps/Input in Cypress/Print credit reports	5%	6					3	3		
Communications with Branches / Depts.	21%	28	5	6	6	6	2.5	2.5		
Writing Tickets/Posting Fees	0%	0					0	0		
Underwriting Analysis	20%	26	5	7	7	7	0	0		
Training	14%	19	7.5	2.5	2.5	2.5	2	2		
Management Functions	4%	5	5							
Misc	2%	2					1	1		
	Total	132	25	21.5	21.5	21.5	21	21	0	0

Function: Indirect Loans		**Hours in .5 hour increments per week**								
Tasks	% of time	Total Hours	Mgr	Cons Ln II	Cons Ln I	Cons Ln II	Cr Asst	Cr Asst	Ln Per	Ln Per
Processing Payments	0%	0								
Customer / Dealer communications	16%	30	2.5	2.5	2.5	2.5	5	5	5	5
Extensions / Loan Modifications	6%	10.5	1.5	1	1	1	3	3		
Audit previous day's fundings	1%	1.5					0.5	1		
Process flooring files	1%	1					1			
Assist Lenders	5%	10					5	5		
Underwriting Analysis / Decision Notification	24%	45.5	3.5	14	14	14				
Training	4%	7.5	2.5	1	1	1	1	1		
Misc	4%	7.5					3.5	4		
Pull Apps/Input in Cypress/Print credit reports	17%	32							16	16
Processing Contracts	7%	14							7	7
Verifying Insurance	2%	4							2	2
Funding Contracts	11%	20							10	10
Management Functions	3%	5	5							
	Total	189	15	18.5	18.5	18.5	19	19	40	40

Fucntion	% of Total Time	Total Hours	Range +- 10%		
Branch Under Writing	**41%**	131.5	37%	45%	**40%**
Indirect Loans	**59%**	188.5	53%	65%	
Total	**100%**	320.0	90%	110%	

Final Cost Allocation

One of the most useful tools to document the appropriate processes is the Work Distribution Chart. The following is offered as a technique for developing such a chart. One is illustrated in the previous Case History.

THE WORK DISTRIBUTION CHART

This chart is a basic tool for identifying work content. It is used to determine:

- The various processes handled by the unit.
- The employees in the unit performing the processes.
- The approximate time spent on the processes by each employee.
- This leads to the identification of the cost of one unit supplying support to other units.

Rules for preparing a work distribution chart

1. Determine the processes in the unit.
2. Write the processes on the chart.

   Categories that are commonly included:
   a. Primary processes
   a. Secondary processes
   b. Supervision
   c. Training (do not include on-job-training)
   d. Special assignments
3. Write names of employees across the top of the chart. Sometimes it is appropriate to substitute position for employees when several employees have same job title; e.g., Teller, File Clerk.
4. Estimate the amount of time each employee or group of employees spend on each process or other category of work each week. If there are processes that do not occur weekly, e.g., monthly or quarterly reports, note these and estimate time required. Perfect accuracy is not expected at this point (any estimate of time less than fifteen minutes is too detailed). This information is best

obtained by interviewing the direct supervisor. It usually takes several iterations because in the first pass you will probably end up with more hours than in the work week. It is important to keep in mind, **record what is happening, not what should happen.**

5. Total the time spent by each employee. It should add to the total working hours during the day or week. If not, re-distribute the time. Total the time spent by employees on each process.
6. Total the time for all processes to obtain the total time spent by the unit.
7. Calculate the percentage of time of the total time each process requires. This should total 100% as printed at the bottom of the form.

Activity Based

www.SimplifiedProfitability.com

CHAPTER 3

SIMPLE ACTIVITY BASED DRIVERS

Once the data is available, this chapter covers how to develop and perform the activity based costing techniques.

From years of experience with small, medium and large institutions we offer Guideline for Classification of Technology Expenses.

In addition, we review the Guideline for Classification of Bookkeeping (Deposit Operations), Item Processing, Core Processing and Network costs.

Finally, we deal with the knotty reality that in some physical locations, there are many responsibility centers. We give examples of how to segregate main office departments, and apply those techniques consistently to other buildings used by multiple responsibility centers.

DEVELOP CHARGE TECHNIQUES

The most frequent Service Centers that require a charge out or internal transfer price within a model are as follows with a suggested unit of measure for a month or a quarter.

Service Center (department)	Driver (basis for charge out)	Unit of measure
1 Core Data Processing	# Active Loan & Deposit accts	$ per account
2 Item Processing	# Demand Deposit accts (active)	$ per account
3 ATM/Debit Processing	# Transaction accounts	$ per account
4 Network	# Workstations (User PC's only)	$ per workstation
5 Loan Ops	# Loan accounts (active)	$ per account
6 Loan Origination	# Loans Closed (during period)	$ per account
7 Deposit Ops	# Deposit accounts (active)	$ per account
8 Occupancy	# Square feet	$ per square ft
9 Other	# of activity	$ per activity

The first four items above are the most complex and critical. Instructions for these three will follow. The remainder follow a simple pattern. Keep in mind that the entire cost accounting model objective is to determine the actual cost during a selected period not what it should be, what we want to be, or what it could be. It is what it is!

Service centers are to be charged out to responsibility centers that are using their services based on selected activities or drivers. Service centers do not carry any general overhead that would be absorbed by profit centers.

Items 5 through 9 above will be determined by their general ledger department expense report. Sometimes a larger department will need to be broken down into the specific service centers defined above. This should include salaries, benefits, depreciation, and general period expenses. Care should be taken not to combine departments that have different drivers. The total cost of the service center for that period is the period cost. The unit of measure equals period cost divided by driver count.

Items 1 through 4 above generally do not have departments identified within the general ledger expense reporting. They are usually to be determined by starting with the combined group of expenses. Cost for these three items: Core, Item, and Networking require an approach that deals with accumulating all three costs and then classifying those costs within this group by line item to the three different service centers.

Each bank will be unique and have a slightly different format due to the nature of the general ledger and of the particular vendors involved. Below is a list of the most likely line item expenses that would have to be dealt with.

Hardware maintenance
Software maintenance
Account processing fee
General ledger expense
Vendor monthly expense
Depreciation
Staff salaries direct
Staff salaries in- direct
Disaster recovery
ATM expenses
ATM/Debt card processing
Telecommunications
Supplies
Misc (contingency)

In order to build this type of ongoing expense classification worksheet it is best to build an appendix for supporting documentation. The suggested headings or worksheet tabs for the appendix are as follows:

Benefits. This worksheet should include all employee related expenses as a percentage of the total salaries of the bank. It does include the bank's share of taxes (employer social security, medicare and unemployment) and Christmas turkeys if appropriate. If a bonus is reported on the employee's W-2 then it is included in the base salaries. It is a bank wide average to simplify calculations and usually runs 20% to 30%.

Salary. In a bank technology group it is rare that one person does one job. This worksheet should assign the percentage that an employee spends in each category. That percent is applied to the base salary plus a benefits ratio.

Fixed assets. The most common first step in addressing Fixed Assets is to get a complete listing of all depreciable assets that have the current book value greater than zero. It is very easy, if a complete listing can be given in an Excel worksheet.

1. Sort the Excel file and eliminate all book value of zero (no depreciation)
2. Copy the results into another tab within the same workbook (to keep an audit trail)
3. Review that and eliminate the obvious line items that have nothing to do with your objective, i.e., buildings, new signs, furniture & fixtures, paintings, etc.
4. Copy the results into another tab within the same workbook (to keep an audit trail)
5. Add a column in the worksheet for classification.
6. Usually it takes several people (at one time) to review the remaining line items and classify them as C=Core, IP=Item Processing, N=Network, and O=Other. Sometimes a few line items require some research.
7. Sort the worksheet on the classification column.
8. Copy the results into another tab within the same workbook (to keep an audit trail)
9. Sum up the period depreciation expense for each category.

Pre-paid. Similar to Fixed Assets except there are fewer items to classify and it usually only covers the current year. Be sure to determine the correct period expense (month or quarter).

Vendor(s) annual maintenance. Refer to invoices(s) for $ and account counts.

Vendor(s) account processing. Refer to invoices(s) for $ and account counts.

Vendor(s) monthly expense. Refer to invoices(s) for $ and account counts.

Vendor(s) ATM expense. Refer to invoices(s) for $ and account counts.

Vendor(s) ATM debit card monthly expense. Refer to invoices(s) for $ and account counts.

General ledger expense. If you have this by core, items, and network wonderful. The author has never found this to be true. It usually has to be constructed. The following two applications can be a valuable source of information.

Bank accounts payable history. Usually available (even if manual in a spreadsheet)

Vendors accounts receivable history. This may (or may not) be available from the vendor.

The most common first step in addressing accounts payable or accounts receivable history is to get a complete listing of all line items during the selected period. It is very easy if a complete listing can be given in an Excel worksheet.

1. Sort the Excel file by *description* first and *date* second.
2. Copy the results into another tab within the same workbook (to keep an audit trail)
3. Review that and eliminate the obvious line items that have nothing to do with your objective.
4. Copy the results into another tab within the same workbook (to keep an audit trail)
5. Add a column in the worksheet for classification.
6. Usually it takes several people (at one time) to review the remaining line items and classify the as C=core, IP=item processing, N=network, and O=other. Sometimes a few line items require some research.
7. Sort the worksheet on the classification column.
8. Copy the results into another tab within the same workbook (to keep an audit trail)
9. Sum up the period depreciation expense for each category.

Examples of actual Appendices are provided. Keep in mind that each bank will have a unique Appendix and final on-going expenses for the period expense. The total cost of the service center (core, items, and network) for that period is the *period cost*. The unit of measure equals period cost divided by driver count.

GUIDELINE FOR CLASSIFICATION OF TECHNOLOGY EXPENSES

The following information is meant to provide a guideline for classification of expenses of technology. The sources for these expenses are Prepaid Expenses, Fixed Assets, and General Ledger expenses.

Prepaid expenses

Prepaid expenses are payments that are set up to be amortized over the life of the asset. We are looking for the monthly expense. Mapping to the proper general ledger expense department is the key. Pre-pays can be in Core Processing, Item Processing or Network.

Fixed assets

Fixed assets have a monthly or annual depreciation expense that must be mapped to the using department. Fixed assets can be in Core Processing, Item Processing or Network. The first step in classifying fixed assets is to eliminate all items that have no book value. The second step would be to identify all branch or non-technical assets. With respect to branches, the hardware/software that is associated with network and the servers and any other equipment that provides a delivery system for the branch becomes Network. Where there is a branch capture process specific branch capture stations become part of Item Processing. They replace a central reader sorter.

General Ledger Expenses

These can be in Core Processing, Item Processing, ATM/Debit or Network. These begin with salaries and employee benefits being mapped to the right department, i.e., core processing, item processing or networking. It is possible to use the Accounts Payable System to classify general ledger expenses to the proper department.

Guideline for Classification of Bookkeeping (Deposit Operations), Item Processing, Core Processing and Network

A Work Distribution Chart is the best way to accomplish this, however to expedite things the following functions are generally classified as shown. These are common functions but not all inclusive.

C- Core Processing

- Received and processed ATM and ACH activities
- Account and parameter maintenance
- Security administration
- Receive and process any nightly files
- Daily processing and backups
- System monitoring
- Application PTF's
- Month, quarter, year end and processing
- Update vendor software
- CPU hardware
- Disaster recovery activities
- New release testing and processing
- Vendor liaison & problem solving

BK- Bookkeeping (Deposit Operations)

- Customer contact/service: help face to face or telephone
- Bank employee contact: help face to face or telephone
- Produce management, audit, & regulatory reports
- Perform administrative duties
- Basically using the core loan and deposit system

IP- Items Processing

- Statement printing, collation, stuffing, folding, postage machine
- Anything related to CAR/LAR
    - Reject re-entry (80% CAR success requires 20% re-entry)
- Balancing branches

N- Network

- Anything that supports online workstations
- Devices common to multiple workstations
- Examples include branch servers, application servers, routers, switches, and common software like firewalls and e-mail

SEGREGATE MAIN OFFICE, AND OTHER BUILDINGS USED BY MULTIPLE RESPONSIBILITY CENTERS

Few if any main office branches are completely free standing buildings with no other operations, overhead, or other profit centers (Trust, Investments, Loan origination) within their walls. The total occupancy costs usually result in a single figure that defines all occupancy expense. It probably includes heating and air conditioning the common areas. The easiest way is to find some blueprints of the building(s) and determine the square feet for each area. Otherwise actual measurements must be made. A spreadsheet can be developed to charge each user for their share of the total cost of occupancy based on square footage required for that function.

Case History: Measuring facilities to determine area (square footage) for departments.

Here is a simple approach for any building. The first step is to begin with the total length and total width. As an example a 100' x 200' building is equal to 20,000 sq. ft. area. Then measure each department forgetting about the halls and closets, etc. Next sum up each of the departments. This will be less than the grand total square footage of the building. Increase each department a pro rata amount to bring the sum of the departments to the grand total for the building. This produces an easily understood definition of the area required for each department. The next step is to determine the overall cost of the total building that includes leasehold improvements, depreciation, utilities, insurance, and anything else related to that facility. It is a simple matter then to calculate a cost per square foot per month and then to apply that to the area required for each department or main office among all of the other centralized buildings expenses.

Case History: Dress codes & efficiency in measuring facilities.

There was the case in a very conservative organization that had a very conservative dress code where the bank employees were faced with absolutely no facility blueprints. There were multiple buildings. Some of these buildings were not necessarily of the "office cleanliness" variety. Two of the ladies came to work one day in jeans with a 150 foot tape measure and proceeded to measure all the buildings. Their work was noticed by a very conservative director of the bank. Needless to say, there were many explanations given and it was finally resolved. The job was accomplished.

When faced with not having drawings, a 150 foot tape is sometimes required. A simple trip to the Home Depot or Lowes shows that there are some significant aids for measuring across spaces. One innovative bank employee found a laser measurement tool and used it in a very efficient manner. Another way that many people have solved this problem is to count ceiling tiles. In any event, it takes a creative person to make this an easy task.

Hancock Campus square footage by resposibility center

	Total	Main PC PC 1	Trust PC 55	Loan Ops 60	Resp ctr Deposit Ops 61	Mkt 70	Exec 72	GOH Adm 73
GROUND LEVEL	13,614	7,527	2,373	2,017		944	476	-
LOWER LEVEL	13,556	351	-	-	4,120		-	4,777
DRIVE-UP	467	467	-	-			-	-
GRAND TOTAL	27,637	8,345	2,373	2,017		944	476	4,777
	27,637	8,345	2,373	2,017		944	476	4,777

Chapter 4

Clear Definitions

Chapter 4 defines further the three tier cost accounting terms for the actual cost approach used in Simplified Profitability.

We provide guidance to determine a base period as a starting point for analysis.

There is a brief case study for the senior management meeting to review definitions, progress, and select the base period.

DEFINE COST ACCOUNTING TERMS

Most bankers think in terms of cost as two tiers, Fixed and Variable. Sometimes this is referred to as Direct and Indirect. Many FASB opinions are expressed in that manner. FASB 91 is a case in point. A more workable (and accurate) approach is to go to the Cost Accounting Handbook or an old Cost Accounting text from college days. This author submits that the appropriate approach is a three tiered approach, Direct, Indirect, and General Overhead. It is sometimes referred to as Variable, Variable Overhead, and Fixed Overhead. Basically it is a Standard format. This facilitates the measurement of direct and indirect and the appropriate grouping of general overhead in order to accomplish a "Fully Burdened" cost accounting system that can be balanced to the general ledger.

Refer to initial Cost Accounting Definitions in Chapter 1 and 2, and the diagram on the facing page.

DETERMINE BASE PERIOD

The most common practice is to select a period, usually a month, that is typical of a year. A lot of questions are raised where one has to make assumptions. Following this initial analysis we will seek out more accurate information to be utilized. After doing the development period to create the first period that we wish to analyze, a more extensive detail work can occur to create the first quarter. Care should be taken to not select a period that includes a year-end. That wouldn't be accurate for an average month. Keep in mind that the purpose is to determine the actual cost during a selected month. Also, a period that is selected so far in the past loses the value of a snapshot and working with current information. Additionally, a period should not be selected that has a major system or marketing approach change. All of this requires balance. Select a period that is representative within a typical year.

Case History: Selecting a base period and building the first system report.

One bank chose a particular month. Then the bank decided to look at it again. The reason was they found that by rearranging and adding a few responsibility centers (departments) to their general ledger it would be a lot easier to do the research. They added the appropriate responsibility centers and waited a month before they did their first analysis as part of the development. Once that was accomplished the work to produce the first actual quarter report was a lot easier and more accurate.

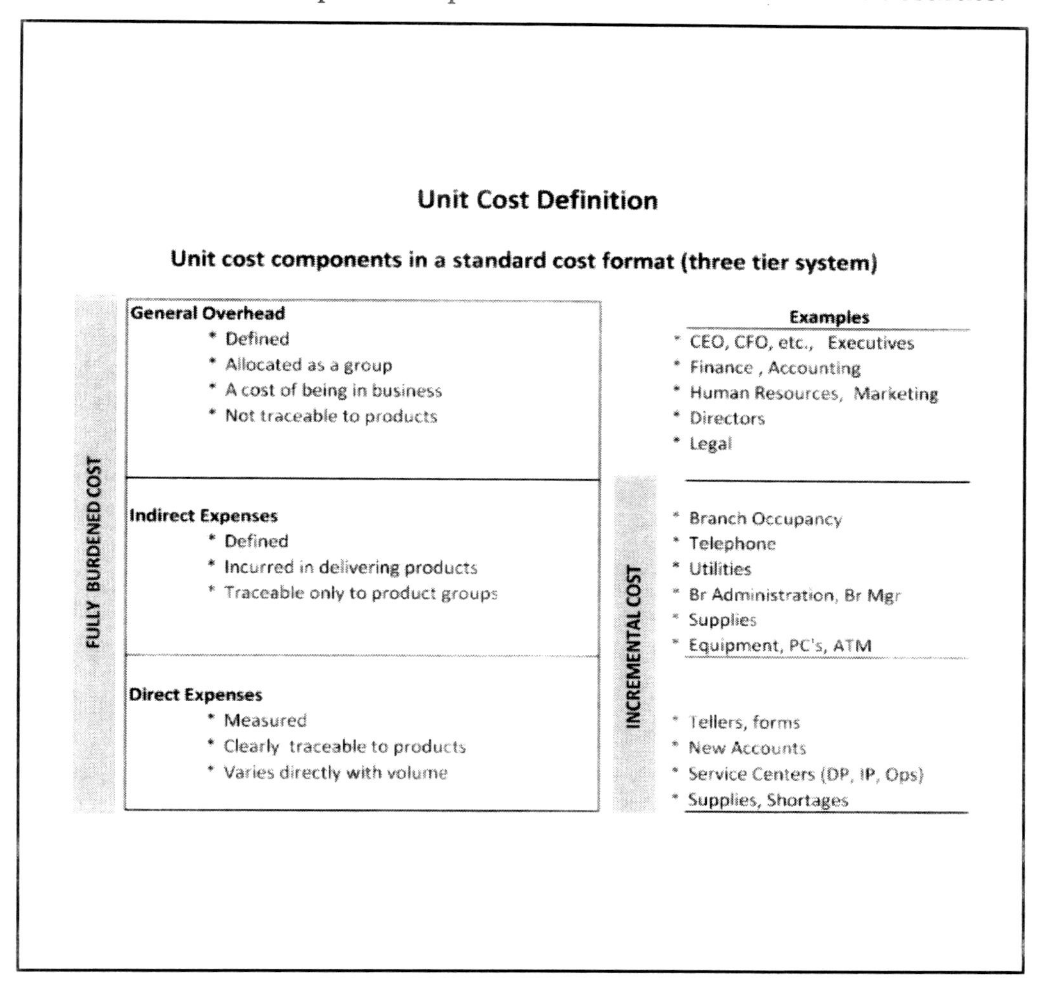

One bank was in a hurry. They had no responsibility centers within the general ledger. They decided to expedite the process. They selected a particular month and then moved to building income and expenses in a massive spreadsheet. This worked (although very labor intensive) with one exception. When they came to working with income areas, they did not take into account the adjustments before books were closed. They had worked with end-of-month reports. As a result when the reports were to be balanced to the general ledger, instead of achieving a 1% variation it was more like 11%. It didn't take long to find out that this was because the significant amount of fees had been waived after closing. Selecting the period has to include knowing if adjustments have been made if going outside the pure general ledger is the method to analyze that period. Note that isolating this large amount of fees being waived had its own benefit.

Case History: An explanation of sequential closeouts (an integral part of cost accounting systems).

One of the most controversial aspects of cost accounting is sequential closeouts. In the early 1980's systems were in place that were arbitrary and their method of charging out very inaccurate. The big problem however, was that cost accounting cost centers would closeout (charge out) to other centers. One of those would then closeout to another. Two other centers would then close out to yet another center. By the time the closeouts or charges would appear on a profit center Income & Expense statement, the poor manager of the profit center had no idea what the charges were for. The author has actually seen nine sequential closeouts in such a system. The objective of a good profitability system should be simple and easily understood. It needs to be noted here that the method (basis) of charging out should not be subjective (arbitrary) percent allocations but based on activities such as accounts or transactions. A diagram of a simple two-step sequential closeout is in Chapter 1.

The objective of the system is to determine the actual cost and profitability of an organization that is fully burdened in a specified period and balanced to the general ledger. This period can be one month, two months or a quarter. It is important to determine the actual cost before attempting to determine what it should cost. Actual cost of a specified period can be accomplished in a short elapsed time frame (before things can change too much).

SENIOR MANAGEMENT MEETING - DEFINITIONS, PROGRESS

Don't wait until the last minute and spring things on senior management. Quite often they will have valuable input, especially with regard to profit center definition.

Case History: If the Senior Management meeting does not include the "C" level officers, time, money, & effort are being wasted!! CEO, CFO, CLO, COO, etc.

Part of the plan of implementation should be 3 to 4 meetings with senior management at the C level. This means Chief Executive Officer, Chief Financial Officer, and Chief Loan Officer etc. The important thing is that the system comes from the top and not just another accounting system. Serious policy decisions such as profit centers, activity based charge out methods, general overhead absorption, funds transfer pricing, etc. are made. Included in the work of implementation are 3 to 4 of these types of meetings with a final meeting before the system is rolled out to the line managers.

Activity Based

www.SimplifiedProfitability.com

Part 2

Management Decides the Foundation

Two Chapters with five work plan steps

Chapter 5 contains detail on the base period and income assignment challenges, while Chapter 6 informs you on the easy to understand, simple yet powerful alternative to identifying general overhead costs.

This part helps you avoid fundamental pitfalls that can doom a profitability project.

Activity Based

www.SimplifiedProfitability.com

Chapter 5

Base Period

At this point we review some fine points with case studies to define income beyond what can be posted to general ledger.

Chapter 5 also addresses the difficulties sorting out and classifying unallocated or miscellaneous costs that may still be included in a general overhead category. These need to be identified to develop base period amounts for Simplified Profitability.

DEFINE INCOME

This is typically more difficult than expenses. Care should be taken to make sure that income figures are not just month-end but include adjustments. In one client we found that 11% of income was adjusted. Needless to say this was an opportunity for improvement. Many fees for deposit service are often not charged to the branch. One answer is to credit this to deposit operations to reduce the expense that will be charged to the branch.

Case History: Determining NSF & OD fees by branch.

Rarely does any bank track NSF overdraft fees to the branch level. A bank wanted to track the NSF and overdraft income fees to the branches. The bank determined that this could not be done historically. All of these income fees were charged to bank level. They determined to put these into a deposit services service center. This reduced the deposit services operating costs. That reduced operating cost was then charged to the branches based on a per account basis. This was not a perfect situation. However, it did allow the branch to benefit from these fees on a pro rata basis. Needless to say, in the future they began to identify these income fees to the branch level.

The choices are to keep the fees centralized and prorate them out through reduction of the expense of the deposits services department, or specifically post the fees to branch responsibility centers in the general ledger.

Case History: Memo posting solves some problems.

Not all income has been booked to profit centers in the general ledger. This can create too much detail and not enough benefit. Take the case of a bank that promoted credit card applications to be taken by the branches. Based on an independent sampling technique or a time ladder the credit card department offered a five dollar incentive to the branches in the profitability system. They just counted the number of applications and put five dollars of income to the branch for each application, then the sum of the branch incentive was expensed in the credit card profit center. This did not have to be posted to the general ledger.

Case History: Creative booking of loans.

A bank in Maryland had an unusual approach. Normally, consumer loans were booked in a branch and commercial loans were booked in a central loan profit center. In this bank, the Senior Loan Officer had a unique approach to motivate branch managers to develop commercial loans as illustrated by the following case. The branch manager had a good relationship with a dry cleaning business over the years. When it came time for that customer to expand and upgrade, the branch manager brought the loan to the bank, even though the central credit and loan operations did all the underwriting. The Senior Loan Officer allowed the loan to be booked in the branch. Obviously, the branch received the interest income. They also got a charge for loan operations and loan servicing. However, the real beneficiary was the bank because no one was concerned about who got the recognition. The important thing was the overall bank performance benefited by the proper use of the system to motivate performance rather than assign blame.

Develop Base Period Amounts

This task depends on the detail of charging departments in the general ledger. Sometimes it is necessary to go to Human Resources in order to get the detail necessary for payroll and fringe benefits. There is usually a hidden monster called ***overhead unallocated*** or some similar name. Quite often it is necessary to dig into the accounts payable system to actually determine where these expenses should be charged for the base period. Obviously more detail and accurate charging is required for the future.

Case History: Untangling unallocated responsibility centers (departments).

A client gave assurances that the general ledger was departmentalized accurately. This was not so. A task to untangle a particular department referred to as unallocated overhead was undertaken. The cost depends on whether Accounts Payable is automated or manual. If manual, determining how to break down and classify entries is a labor-intensive task of going to the physical invoice file. If there is an automated Accounts Payable system, a vendor history for the base period can be run. This really expedites the task. Typically after this exercise, additional departments are added to the general ledger for more detail. Obviously, more attention to accurate charging occurs at the Accounts Payable desk.

Activity Based

www.SimplifiedProfitability.com

CHAPTER 6

GENERAL OVERHEAD METHOD

At this point one of the most important steps is outlined. How you classify general overhead (GOH). Because we have seen common practices that produce poor results we present case studies to prevent wasteful false steps.

This chapter reveals and discusses several GOH allocation alternatives.

A Senior Management Meeting is important at this stage to set the GOH allocation. Then the next important decisions are previewed - the funds transfer calculations.

We provide a detail case history of this important decision meeting.

CLASSIFY GENERAL OVERHEAD (GOH)

Depending on the detail in the general ledger and payroll system this can be relatively simple. It includes such things as executive expense, director's fees, legal fees (not loan related), human resources, finance & accounting, marketing. (Except where advertising can be identified by loan or deposit.)

Case History: Simplification of general overhead.

Historically, most efforts to allocate general overhead included many complex algorithms. Furthermore, the definition of what makes up general overhead varies a great deal.

General overhead is the fixed costs of operating a bank as defined above. It is the ***cost of doing business***.

General overhead should be defined as a summation of its several components. It should be one lump sum.

GOH ALLOCATION ALTERNATIVES

The author has never had a problem explaining to the president that someone has to pay for his salary. Likewise for other general overhead. The trick is to determine a fair way to allocate this amount to each of the profit centers. The author has seen some pretty wild schemes over the years. The most accepted method has been to group the amount of general overhead into one figure. Allocate it only to profit centers, For every dollar of expense incurred in the profit center, a proportionate amount of general overhead is applied. Example: $0.25 of general overhead per $1.00 of non-interest direct & indirect expense.

Case History: How <u>not</u> to allocate general overhead.

Software developers show off their powerful engines and demonstrate that they can allocate general overhead all over the map in ninety-nine different ways.

Accounting purists seek detail to rationalize accuracy. The result is allocation at the ***T account*** level (or groupings) using various allocation algorithms.

Either of these methods complicate the process enormously and achieves no greater accuracy. In fact, it has the opposite effect. It confuses. It creates perfect inaccuracy.

Case History: The evolution of an acceptable method of allocation.

In the days before the current computer systems and the introduction of spreadsheet detail capability, reasonable methods have evolved. The original immediate reaction was to allocate general overhead based on head count. This was always the desire of the loan division because immediately the branch system had to recover 70% or more of the general overhead. Many systems today utilize head count as a means of allocating different expenses, including general overhead. This is easy to get as it is now, but extremely difficult to get in terms of budgeting for the next period or the next year.

Experience shows that the most equitable and predictable method or algorithm to allocate general overhead is for each one dollar of the bank's non interest expense, there is an amount of general overhead that is recovered. In the example above it is $0.25 of general overhead for each $1.00 of non interest direct and indirect expense.

This is not a negotiable rate, but set by senior management policy.

SENIOR MANAGEMENT MEETING - GOH ALLOCATION

At this point in the profitability model project we meet with senior management to discuss and choose the allocation method for general overhead costs. The planned agenda requires up to two hours discussion using the actual model as set up for the base month or quarter. We calculate the effects of the alternative allocation methods being considered. Everyone sees the effects of the alternatives.

This and other senior management meetings are an integral part of the Simplified Organization Profitability System. It provides ***buy-in*** and makes it a management system and not an accounting system.

Agenda

1. Review project progress to date, and any outstanding issues
2. Trace the source elements of general overhead costs and gain
3. Discuss two to three alternative allocation methods with some variations
4. Choose the general overhead allocation method for this bank
5. Preview the next step – determining the Funds Transfer Rate

Objectives

Simplified organizational profitability includes the objective for general overhead allocation to be easily understood and fair for all the profit centers. RMA has found that a single, simple allocation of the entire pool of general overhead costs helps ensure buy-in of everyone responsible for improving performance.

Alternatives - pros and cons

- Head count
- Number of accounts
- Total account balances
- Number of customers
- Total direct and indirect expense excluding general overhead
- Non interest expense

Preview Funds Transfer Rate (FTR)

After the decision is made on the general overhead allocation method, in this meeting, we preview the discussion topic that will be addressed in the next senior management session. We define the calculation of the funds transfer rate that will be used in the simplified organizational profitability model to determine the credit to a profit center for funds brought into the pool, and to determine charges on use of the pool funds for loans and investments.

Funds pool concept

We briefly review the evolution of funds transfer, including the historical methods of net funds suppliers and net funds users, the term and rate methods developed for asset liability management, and the marginal cost pricing techniques developed for lending.

Once again, we reinforce the advantages of using a simple pool concept for the purposes of organizational profitability measurement. Please refer to the diagrams in chapter 7.

Store manager approach

We conclude the senior management general overhead allocation meeting with acknowledgment that the decisions support the objective to fairly and completely recover overhead costs from all the profit centers, with an easy-to-understand method applied consistently to all the branches and profit generating teams. We want each profit center leader, even deposit only branches, to behave as store managers, excited and encouraged to make their stores high performers including their share of the overhead, what might be viewed as a franchise cost.

Case History

We met one summer morning with the president and chief financial officer and the chief lending officer. Two analysts from the accounting group had prepared and entered the model base information. One of the analysts had led the task to identify the occupancy and network drivers for all the profit centers, service centers, and the general overhead responsibility centers. That task work had prepared him well for the discussion, as he had talked with many of the profit center managers that worked in shared location space in branches and operations buildings.

The discussion began with a brief review of RMA experience over decades working with community banks across the nation to determine an easy to understand and fair method of allocating general overhead.

We discussed the disadvantages of several methods. For example, head count will unfairly charge more overhead cost to the deposit and branch organizations, than to lending. Likewise, using the number of customers or number of accounts would clearly have the same unfair effect.

During the meeting, the management team reviewed, in some depth, each branch situation. All the older, more established branches generate a higher return on occupancy and network expenses. Newer branches, on the other hand, can easily be described as not mature, not yet generating and supporting all the customers, accounts, transactions, and balances they are designed for.

We went through the advantages of using non interest expense as the allocating driver for general overhead. Because non interest expense includes the costs that are directly controllable by profit center managers, there is an incentive to manage those costs effectively, and thereby receive a relatively lower portion of the general overhead allocations. So, by using non interest expense to allocate general overhead, the bank gains by encouraging cost control.

However, at this bank, the management team decided to use a modified non interest expense to allocate general overhead. They will exclude occupancy costs, because branch to branch, in their different markets, the underlying commercial real estate costs per square foot vary so much, and that expense variation is outside the control of the profit center manager.

By modifying the non interest expense allocation method in this way, senior management will focus profit centers cost control more sharply.

Author's note: This was an unusual decision to exclude occupancy expense from the basis to recover general overhead. More than ninety percent of clients have historically chosen total non-interest expense as the basis for recovery.

Part 3

Set Funds Transfer Rate

This is the most controversial part. Two Chapters with three work plan steps are covered.

Chapter 7 includes a conceptual introduction and examples of a unique and powerful approach to the challenge of determining an accurate, fair and practical true cost of funds. The Simplified Profitability effectiveness is built on a foundation that all financial institution people can understand and accept, especially those without an accounting background.

Chapter 8 contains the road map to gaining management commitment and confidence in both the funds transfer rate and the overall integrity of the Simplified Profitability framework.

Activity Based

www.SimplifiedProfitability.com

CHAPTER 7

FUNDS PROVIDED EARNINGS & FUNDS USED CHARGES

Chapter 7 shows how to accomplish the first step, to identify the True Cost of Funds.

We review the evolution of Funds Transfer Pricing (FTP) to set the stage for the unique Simplified Profitability method. Several diagrams help visualize this challenging subject.

Finally we offer a caution - **Transferring Funds Costs is not Product Pricing!**

TRUE COST OF FUNDS

The author has heard many arguments for multiple pools of funds when trying to make an asset/liability management system rather than performing cost accounting. After many arguments the use of a single pool of funds based on average cost and including the ***cost to secure*** works best the first time around.

Sometimes, clients have made some modifications to this when going into product cost accounting but always tied back to the single pool in aggregate.

Case History: The evolution of Funds Transfer Pricing (FTP)

- 1960's - The banks used net supplier / net user of funds as a basis for profitability analysis
- 1980's - The banks started serious use of asset/liability management systems and this became one basis for profitability analysis
- 1990's - The banks confused matched fund pricing with cost accounting & profitability analysis
- 21st Century - A few banks began to approach profitability analysis with ***activity based cost accounting*** and internal funds transfer method based on the ***True Cost of Funds*** and balancing to the general ledger and the financial statements.

Bankers are hung up on traditional methods of Funds Transfer Pricing. As such they can only come close to balancing to the general ledger by creating a ***dummy*** center. You can't be out of balance when you can plug.

Illustration: Funds Transfer Method Monograph

The objective of the RMA profitability system is to achieve accuracy to general ledger within ± 5%. This is in keeping with the typical objective of a standard cost system in a manufacturing or retail environment that has an accuracy objective of perfection but recognizes, as a practical matter, it would be within plus or minus 5%. Bankers have difficulty with this concept. Banks typically balance to the penny, whereas cost accounting recognizes the practicality of the cost of measurement exceeding the value of the cost determination. So a certain amount of latitude is required in a standard cost system. When actual is compared to standard and the variance is equal to or greater than 5% (favorable or unfavorable) then a variance analysis is performed.

A common misdirection many banks take is the use of asset liability management systems. It is desirable to match funds and to have rate risk analysis (rate shock.) However, inventory control is nothing more than one component of the total profitability of an organization. Several authors of these types of systems have agreed that asset liability management and cost accounting and profitability analysis, although they are complementary, they are not necessarily dependent. Many banks try to incorporate matched funds with cost accounting and profitability. It has application, but not dependency.

An important step that is often overlooked is that any profitability reporting system must balance to the general ledger. The general ledger is fundamental to business and the source of all financial statements that are received by investors and regulatory agencies. The general ledger and a profitability system produce a snapshot of what is happening during the period reported, be it a month, quarter, or year. Any system that does not balance to the general ledger has its own pitfalls. Any variance analysis, such as rate/volume, rising/falling rate scenario, credit decisions of the past are merely an explanation of why that snapshot says what it does. The profitability system snapshot itself must be balanced to the general ledger. It is what it is.

The first step in developing a funds transfer method is to review the source of funds. The RMA system approaches this from the viewpoint of a manufacturing company. To simplify a manufacturing model:

- Money is the raw material.
- Branches secure the money.
- Money is then "sold" to borrowers or invested in securities.

Refer to page 68 and 69 for two Internal Funds Transfer Rate diagrams - starting with the first step flow chart which illustrates how the Funds Earnings Credit is determined based on the True Cost of Funds.

A myth that software vendors have promoted is as many as 99 pools of funds are needed in a system to be accurate. This conclusion comes from trying to match funds with product life. This is not a practical matter in profitability analysis. Matching funds may be for pricing purposes but do not confuse profitability analysis with pricing products!

Lets go through all the elements of the Simplified Profitability funds transfer rate calculations starting at the top. The sources of funds are branch deposits, borrowed money, escrow and capital.

The branch is a source of funds that has an expense associated with it other than just the cost of money (interest cost.) This is the cost to secure funds. The direct and indirect expense and a fair share of allocation of general overhead make up the cost to secure. If you take the interest cost (in basis point comparison) and add to that the direct, indirect, and general overhead costs for a branch or group of branches (converted to basis points as a function of the deposits gathered) you will come up with the true cost of funds. In simple terms interest paid plus costs to secure with a fair share of overhead allocated is the True Cost of Funds.

The true cost of funds for borrowed money is the interest expense paid. All we have to do is go to a borrowing window and get that money, but we pay a higher interest rate.

The interest cost for escrow is a unique situation and very low (sometimes zero). This is where a bank would be holding escrow funds as it relates to a lending or deposit product, i.e. residential mortgage, or law firm escrows.

Occasionally a bank will have excess capital. This means that the heavily capitalized institution has funds available for the pool to lend or invest. These funds would be available at zero expense. This calculation using capital has nothing to do with any calculation that determines regulatory requirements of capital ratios.

The funds earning credit for branches that provide funds to the pool is a very important part of the total system. If we buy the funds from the branches at the True Cost of Funds in aggregate for all the branches, the branches would only break even. (Excluding loan or deposit fees, such as NSF charges or safe deposit box fees, etc.) It's important that we include funds gathering managers as profit centers managers.

Therefore, we add a branch incentive that is determined by experience and management judgement over time and typically ranges between 10 and 100 basis points. Market rates that are very low would justify a lower branch incentive margin like 10 basis points, while in a high rate market an appropriate incentive margin might be 50 basis points or higher.

Choose a good place to start based on current rates to set the true cost of funds for the funds earning credit/funds use cost, overall - the funds transfer rate. This way a funds supplying center is profitable, if they meet their goals for mix of products and rates plus achieving some fees. They become a true profit center.

Peg Rate is a true aggregate rate. It is made up of the rate the bank is paying to secure funds and the rate the bank is charging for the use of those funds. If it is necessary because of large multiple market places you could have a maximum of four different true cost of funds based on different metropolitan or multi-county markets. These must all be blended into one peg rate. An example would be a state or a multi-state market that had several metropolitan and competitive markets. The true cost of funds would vary between markets. The peg rate then becomes an aggregate of all sources, which becomes the same aggregate (or peg rate) for all uses.

The first diagram on the following two facing pages represents the complete flow in calculating the Internal Funds Transfer Rate. This model works whether the profit center is a supplier only, user only, or a mix of both. There is no ***net*** user/supplier. Calculation of True Cost of Funds includes only deposits gathered in branches.

The second diagram illustrates how investments and lending use the pool as a source of funds. Notice that if the funds use charge is set lower for investments, you must set the funds use charge higher for loans. The weighted average for investments and lending must equal the Peg Rate so the profitability system will balance to the general ledger.

The funds use charge is for those earning assets (loans, investments) that use the funds. In this system a profit center could be a funds supplier only, a funds user only, or both. Most banks begin with one funds use charge for simplicity (this is the average or peg rate.) If it is necessary because of diverse earning assets there could be different funds use charges. An example would be commercial loans, consumer loans, residential loans, and investments. These must all be blended back to one peg rate.

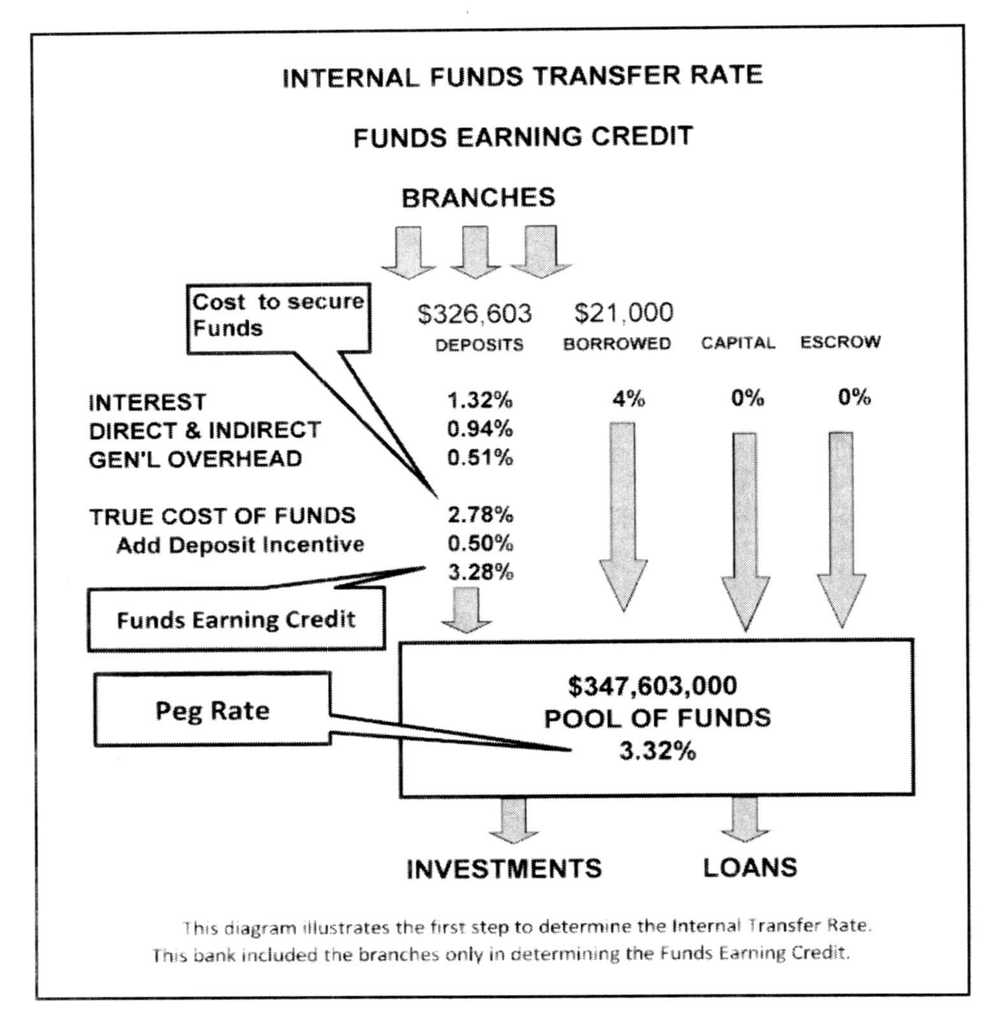

This diagram illustrates the first step to determine the Internal Transfer Rate.
This bank included the branches only in determining the Funds Earning Credit.

The most important thing is, no matter how it's perceived there must be a Peg Rate, the *internal transfer rate*. The Peg Rate is the weighted average of the costs of all sources of funds.

It is important that we use the Peg Rate as the basis for the funds use charge. Notice in all of the steps that we are describing we are trying to balance back to the general ledger and balance within the system.

There is no incremental analysis without considering the whole picture.

Now lets look at an actual bank's situation. Notice that the first diagram on the next page is more complicated than the conceptual exam-

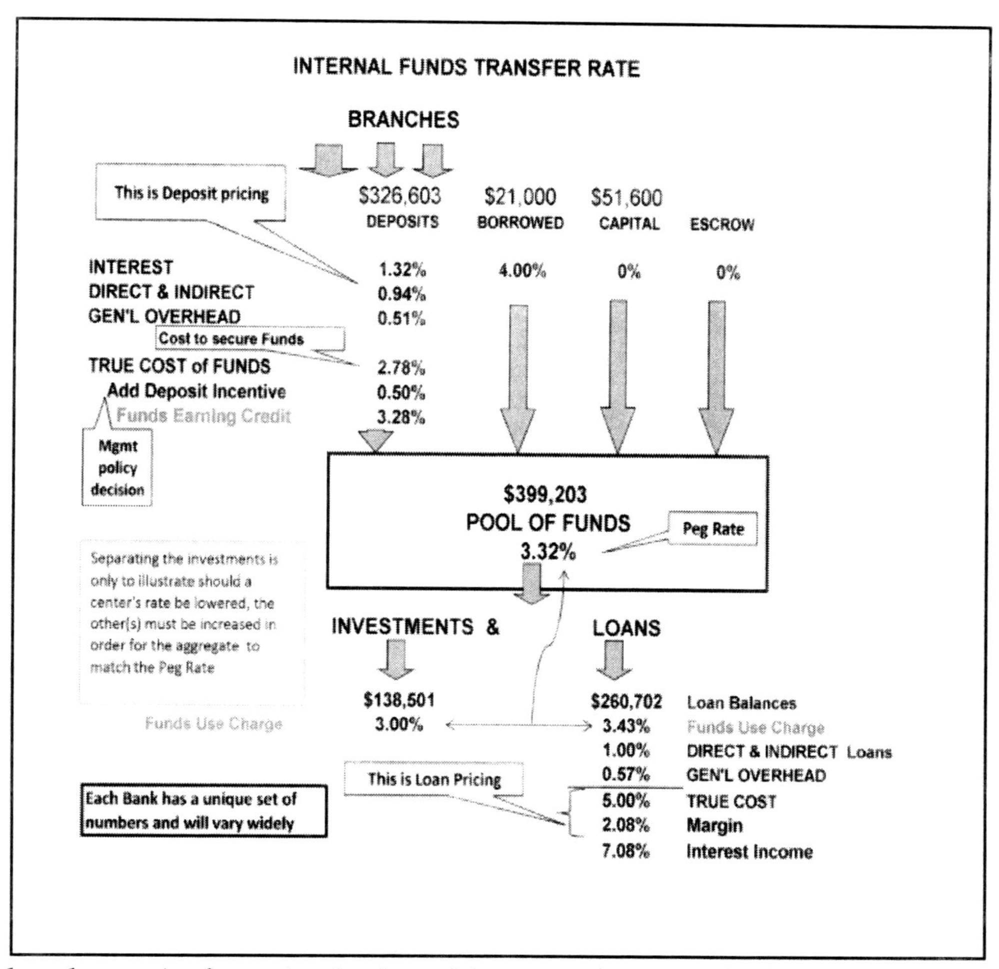

ples above. At the point in time this example was calculated, their pool of funds included borrowed money and capital as well as deposits. You can see that the overall deposit interest costs are quite low, and also that their judgement of a useful branch incentive was correspondingly low too.

The calculation example reveals exactly how the funds transfer rate was determined. At this bank the Simplified Profitability model balanced to the general ledger within less than a 1% difference.

In summary, the funds transfer mechanism is probably the most important and yet one of the most misunderstood. Notice that there was little confusion about measuring the direct and indirect costs of securing funds. Sound work measurement approaches introduce a quantified (activity) based cost accounting system. It eliminates *negotiated costs*.

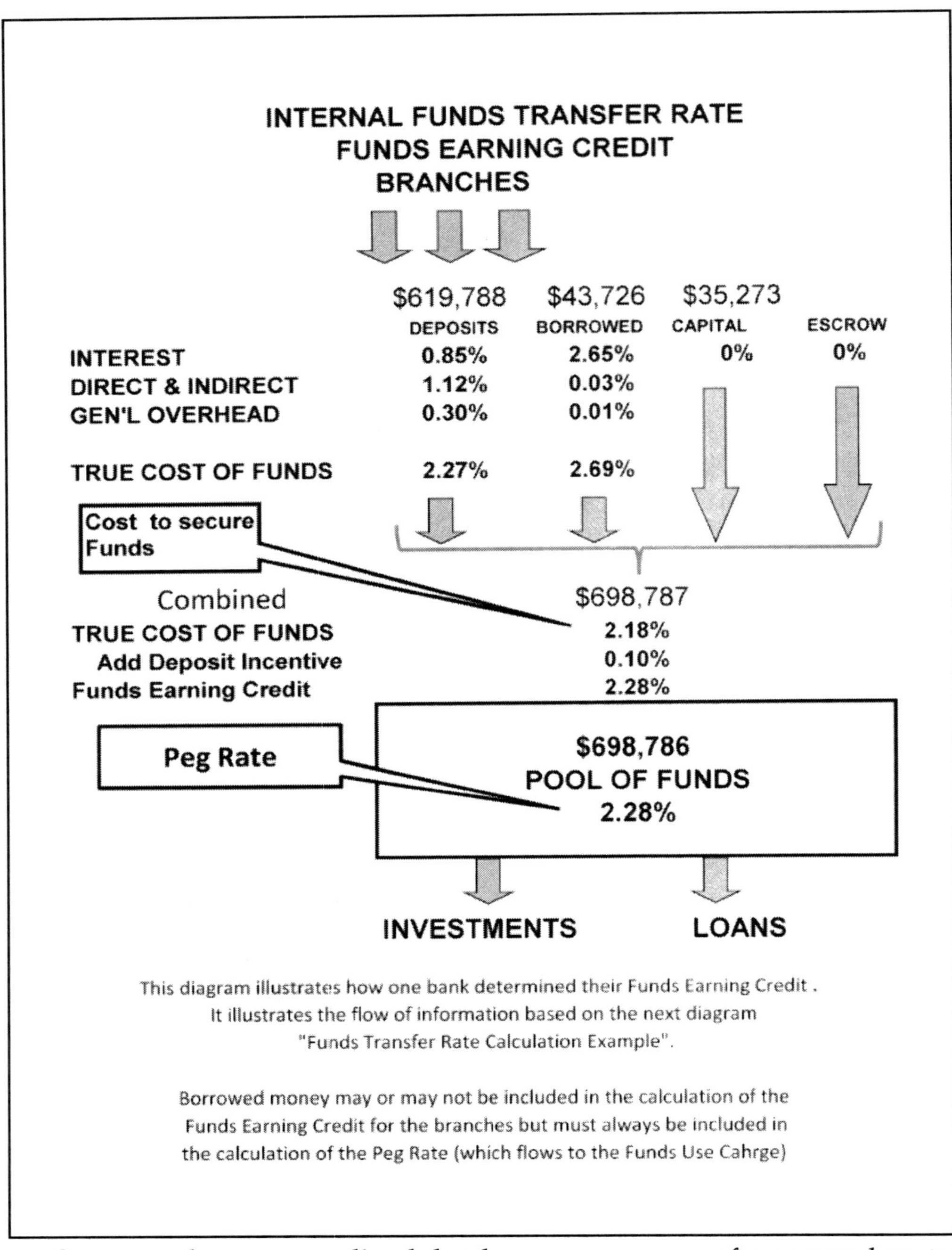

This diagram illustrates how one bank determined their Funds Earning Credit. It illustrates the flow of information based on the next diagram "Funds Transfer Rate Calculation Example".

Borrowed money may or may not be included in the calculation of the Funds Earning Credit for the branches but must always be included in the calculation of the Peg Rate (which flows to the Funds Use Cahrge)

Some use large generalized databases as a source of measured costs. An example would be the old Federal Reserve Functional Cost database or some current independent consultant's database. When it comes to funds transfer mechanism there are many opinions.

Funds Transfer Rate Calculation Example

Organization Cost & Profitability Analysis — Period QTR4, 2012

Used Capital & Other Investable Liabilities

Deposits & Borrowings	663,512,334	
Loans & Investments	698,786,629	
Capital Used (If positive)	35,273,295	(at zero cost)

(If negative : Deposits & Borrowings Not used) Assigned to Investments Profit Center

Br #	Deposits	%	Capital Used based on Deposits %	Total Used Pool of Funds	Cost of Funds	FDIC cost %	Direct & Indirect cost %	GOH cost %	True Cost of Funds Used
01	101,538,043	16.4%	5,778,723	107,316,766	0.72%	0.22%	0.79%	0.28%	2.01%
02	15,140,665	2.4%	861,684	16,002,349	0.86%	0.23%	1.29%	0.45%	2.84%
03	37,519,870	6.1%	2,135,327	39,655,197	0.85%	0.20%	1.06%	0.37%	2.49%
04	45,423,549	7.3%	2,585,140	48,008,689	0.68%	0.22%	0.79%	0.28%	1.98%
05	10,816,115	1.7%	615,566	11,431,680	0.58%	0.21%	2.65%	0.94%	4.39%
06	32,217,340	5.2%	1,833,550	34,050,890	1.22%	0.22%	0.91%	0.31%	2.66%
07	154,373,431	24.9%	8,785,685	163,159,116	0.74%	0.22%	0.27%	0.10%	1.33%
08	14,041,154	2.3%	799,109	14,840,263	0.82%	0.23%	1.44%	0.48%	2.96%
10	38,333,580	6.2%	2,181,637	40,515,217	0.93%	0.23%	0.79%	0.26%	2.19%
20	77,358,790	12.5%	4,402,636	81,761,426	0.78%	0.22%	0.75%	0.25%	1.99%
21	9,131,299	1.5%	519,680	9,650,978	0.82%	0.22%	3.23%	1.01%	5.29%
40	22,540,846	3.6%	1,282,842	23,823,688	1.05%	0.22%	1.43%	0.43%	3.14%
43	3,830,660	0.6%	218,010	4,048,670	1.58%	0.05%	0.55%	0.22%	2.41%
50	57,522,345	9.3%	3,273,706	60,796,050	0.73%	0.22%	1.33%	0.43%	2.71%
42	43,725,649		-	43,725,649	2.65%	0.00%	0.03%	0.01%	2.69%
41			0	-					
	663,513,334	100%	35,273,295	698,786,629	0.92%	0.21%	0.79%	0.27%	2.18%

42 Borrowings
41 Investments

Percentages (%) are calculated based on Total Used Pool of Funds

TRUE COST OF FUNDS USED	**2.18%**	
ADD - BRANCH INCENTIVE	**0.10%**	
INTERNAL TRANSFER RATE	**2.28%**	**ANNUAL**

4.05%	*From another*
0.50%	*example from*
4.55%	*QTR2, 2002*

This diagram illustrates the calculations involved in determining the Funds Transfer Rate based on the True Cost of Funds.

Essentially, a profitability system measures the profitability during a specified period and must balance to the general ledger. All other issues are nothing more than variance analysis, condition analysis, or rationalization that describes why we are where we are.

Beware of the system that requires setting up a *dummy center* (sometimes called Treasury) in order to balance to the general ledger. This just hides the true profitability contribution. It creates a relative profitability rather than an absolute profit contribution. For example, we observed in a very large bank, which was marginally profitable that all forty six branches showed a substantial profit. The Treasury department was the big loser!

The objective of the Simplified Profitability system is to develop an absolute profit contribution and achieve accuracy within ± 5%. We often achieve a greater degree of accuracy.

Insuring that the profitability system balances to the general ledger is an extremely important part of this whole process. It is best to begin any balancing by using income before taxes. (Taxes have their own world.) Balance the total income in the profitability system to the total income from the general ledger. This would include both interest and non interest income. The same can occur for balancing the expenses to the general ledger.

The funds transfer pricing methodology should be viewed as one component of a Profitability Measurement System. That system must meet the following test: the sum of the profit centers' profit or loss must equal the consolidated general ledger income before taxes +/- 5%. Experience has shown that an accuracy of +/- 1% can be achieved.

It is a practical matter that the total funds earning credit and the total fund use charge will never perfectly equal. This is because the total amount of funds used is never equal to the total amount of funds available. Many software companies have spent a fortune trying to make this balance perfectly by creating complex algorithms that worked on average daily balances.

The Simplified Profitability System does not need to include cash and equivalents, balancing the difference in accounts payable and accounts receivable, or accrual variations that occur. By ensuring that fund transfer includes all the deposits, borrowings, escrow and capital used to fund the earning assets of loans and investments, the system balances to within 1% of interest income and expense. Although it's not perfect, it is a valid basis for management decisions .

Case History: Practical examples of balancing to the General Ledger

In one case, the income before taxes was 11% high meaning that the system had recovered 11% more than the general ledger had shown. Investigation showed that they had used the general ledger before adjustments as their source of balancing. That is when the bank realized that a significant amount of fees were being waived. Eventually this was brought down to within 1% after several periods of education.

In another case, the funds earning credit and the funds use charge were 1.3% different. Further examination showed that the cash and equivalents were more than 3% of assets. This was a bank that was carrying excess cash in the branches.

An important practical observation has been that any profit center is rarely changed from loser to winner by increasing its income or reducing its expenses by one or two percent. Essentially that rare profit center is truly a break even center. These are indeed very rare.

The cost of perfection is great. The time required for perfection usually means that by the time results are reported, things have changed.

TRANSFERRING FUNDS COSTS IS NOT PRODUCT PRICING

The funds transfer method described in the previous chapter is a dramatic departure from the bankers experience because everyone traditionally thinks of deposit and loan product pricing. Deposit pricing is what is being put into the pool of funds at a given time and generates expense over a period of time. Loan pricing is what is being taken from the pool of funds at a given time and generates income over a period of time.

The funds transfer method outlined in this book allows the measurement of the bank's profitability at a given time that includes all past product pricing of deposits and loans, all bad deposit charge-offs, and credit losses incorporated in a period's profitability statement. Results of poor management and bad management are displayed. Effects of good markets and bad markets, rising and falling rates, etc. are all a part of it. **It is what it is**!

The funds transfer method and the total profitability measurement system contain valuable components for the deposit and loan pricing. As an example, most loan pricing systems on the market would benefit greatly if they had the service center charge out developed in this system. Another way to look at this is to recognize the deposit or loan pricing supplies or uses funds on a specific day. Each decision affects only a small part of the total population of the pool of funds and the banks P&L for a selected month, quarter, or year.

Surely the bank must manage the asset liability mix, good fiduciary responsibility in supplying funds, excellent risk management, compliance with the regulatory requirements, and many other requirements and restraints. The approach outlined in this book captures the results contributed by each component organization of the total bank and balances (within reason) to the general ledger and financial reports to the stockholders and regulatory authorities. There are no *dummy profit centers*, no *forced balancing*, or no *plugged numbers*. **It is what it is!**

Loan and deposit pricing are a completely different subject!! Competitive forces and relationship value are more important in pricing than costs. After all, your customers do not care what your costs are, just what your products and services provide in competitive value to them.

Chapter 8

Senior Management Meeting - Balancing & Buy-In

For this critical meeting we show a typical Agenda. This includes a review of the balancing proof. And the calculation worksheets that determine the funds transfer rate.

Then an extensive case study is described. And then, we explain the formula that ensures Simplified Profitability credibility.

All this is accomplished without resorting to a dummy account to force balance back to the general ledger.

At this stage of the Simplified Profitability implementation, another senior management meeting is scheduled to review and make final decisions on an effective funds transfer rate. This rate becomes the foundation for calculating the credit for funds secured into the pool, and the charge for funds used from the pool for loans and investments.

Prior to the senior management meeting on the funds transfer rate, the simplified profitability analysts complete a proof worksheet. The setup sheet and the service center worksheets include totals that balance back to the general ledger and other primary sources such as payroll. The proof sheet balances the setup worksheet and the service center sheets both to the funds transfer worksheet and individual and summary profit center reports.

Another way to describe control structure is to say that the input is balanced to the financial and processing sources, and the model processes are balanced to the output, the profit center reports. This input-process-output balancing ensures the integrity of the profitability model.

Here's a typical agenda for this senior management meeting:

Agenda

Objectives – A fair and common sense way to calculate credit and charges for funds, and an incentive for profit center managers that primarily supply funds.

Model Proof – Balancing to general ledger income and expense and balancing the model processes to the output profitability reports.

Capital - as a source of funds and other sources, such as escrow balances.

Single peg rate - for calculating both credit for funds supplied and charges for funds used.

Branch incentive decision - based on current market rates.

Preview Management meeting & Rollout - the final steps in implementing simplified organizational profitability.

Case Study - Model proof and balancing foundation for Senior Management Funds Transfer Rate credibility

Building a Simplified Profitability model that balances to the financial records requires some pragmatic decisions and methods. At most of our bank clients, for example, interchange income on ATM/debit cards can not easily be posted directly to the profit centers. Instead, this non interest income is posted to a service center, and then distributed to the profit centers with an activity-based driver.

Since this step is accomplished within a model process, the proof worksheet must include calculations that reflect this method of distributing the interchange income. Otherwise the process proof will not balance.

Another example was how we handled income from exception items services performed in deposit operations. This income could not be identified by profit center. Because the amounts were small within the service center worksheet before applying the activity based driver we netted out these fees against the total service center costs.

The greatest challenge, however, was in balancing the effects of using the funds transfer rate to calculate credit for funds supplied, and charges for funds used. The preliminary version of the funds transfer worksheet included only deposits and borrowings. The proof worksheet was significantly out of balance.

If the sum of deposit and borrowing average balances exactly equals the sum of loan and investment average balances, then the total calculated credit for funds supplied will exactly equal the total charges for funds used in all profit centers.

Just like every other financial institution, at the example bank this equilibrium did not exist. In fact, the total of loans and investments significantly exceeded the total of their deposits and borrowings. This is not an unusual condition for any financial institution. Even the opposite situation, where deposits and borrowings are greater than loans and investments, is possible.

Just as loan to deposit ratios are never exactly 100%, interest-earning assets will never be exactly equal to interest-bearing liabilities.

So, how can the Simplified Profitability model balance overall? The answer is common sense.

The difference in funds comes from capital, when loans and investments exceed deposits and borrowings. Where else could the money come from? In this bank there were no escrow balances. FED funds bought and sold were included in the Investments and Borrowings profit centers.

The funds transfer rate worksheet calculates and accounts for the use of capital in the pool. Because our goal is to balance the profit model to the actual income and expense posted in general ledger, we assign a zero cost to the capital used. After all, there's no cost of capital posted as an expense in general ledger.

Here's the general formula: **L + I + FFS = D + B + E + FFB + C**

Loans + Investments + Fed Funds Sold = Deposits + Borrowings + Escrow + Fed Funds Bought + Capital.

Simplified Profitability includes this common sense truism in the Funds Transfer Rate worksheet, and this easy to understand approach is one of the keys to balancing organizational profitability to the general ledger. (Without resorting to a force balancing account often labeled *Treasury*.)

Part 4

Make It Happen - Drive Results

Part 4 focuses on results and analysis so management can identify the most profitable and practical actions, and then see how the financial institution is improving profits period by period.

First, you determine *What to change,* then you will find ideas and guidance on *How to change.*

Part 4 contains three chapters, with two work plan steps and a summary with an entire work plan example.

Chapter 9 walks you through the production and assembly steps and illustrates with examples the power of a simple one page profit center report format.

Chapter 10 is a road map with examples of the use of the Simplified Profitability output with management engagement to focus on improvement plans that will move the performance needle.

Chapter 11 recaps the entire Simplified Profitability process with step by step summaries.

Activity Based

www.SimplifiedProfitability.com

CHAPTER 9

ASSEMBLE PROFITABILITY REPORTS & ANALYZE RESULTS

In this chapter we present examples of final reports. These reflect the essential value of Simplified Profitability. And we discuss the inherent flexibility of our approach.

For example, we review two recent additions driven by the economic challenges experienced in the last few years. The examples break out the *FDIC assessment*, and *Contribution to Loan Loss*.

Obviously the RMA Excel model can facilitate producing the profit & loss Statement for each profit center. The most common question is how long does it take? That depends on the number of responsibility centers. For an average community bank (less than $400 million) it might take 2 to 3 days the first time around given that the above steps are completed. Thereafter, the work takes less than a half day per period. A quarter is recommended. The author has one client that loads the model and balances in less than 15 minutes. It all depends on how the general ledger is set up.

Case History: Examples of final report.

The following are examples of the most common reports that have been produced:

- Example National Bank Branch 07
- Blank Bank & Blank Branch
- Summary report of five branch region
- Summary report of five commercial loan offices

The newest expense line added is the *FDIC assessment* which is truly a direct expense based on deposits. Another line item in the analysis is *Contribution to Loan Loss* which is an expense. (Usually allocated to profit centers based on charge off expense.) Some loan officers confuse Contribution, which is an expense, and individual loan Charge-offs against the Loan Loss Reserve. They really get confused about recoveries. (Which go back to reserves.) The author suggests an accounting 101 refresher.

Several clients have asked for different line items to be added. That is probably good as long as it makes sense and still results in a ONE PAGE REPORT in 12 point type. Do not put the Declaration of Independence on a pin head. It cannot be read!

Example National Bank

Organization Cost & Profitability Analysis

Period: Jan-Mar 2011

		Branch 07
Total Deposits		$ 13,247,287
Available Capital		$ 839,276
Total Gross Loans		$ 4,529,449
Income		
	Deposit Fees	$ 14,134
	Loan Fees	$ 3,712
	Interest	$ 73,134
	Funds earning credit	$ 153,590
	Total	$ 244,570
Expenses		
	Direct & Indirect	$ 34,178
	FDIC Assesment	$ 5,630
	Service center charges	
	Data Processing	$ 5,280
	Deposit Ops	$ 10,055
	Items Processing	$ 2,232
	Loan Operations	$ 7,056
	Network	$ 2,560
	Branch Admin	$ 1,858
	Operations Admin	$ 2,055
	Interest Expense	$ 49,532
	General Overhead	$ 13,600
	Funds use charge	$ 49,386
	Total	$ 183,422
Net Profit		$ 61,148
	Contribute to Loan Loss	$ 3,079
Profit after LL		$ 58,068

Bank Name

Organization Cost & Profitability Analysis

Period	4th Qtr '10		
		Office Name	
		Resp Ctr No.	
Total Deposits		$	44,907,357
Available Capital			
Total Gross Loans		$	386,903
Income			
	Deposit Fees	$	6,630
	Loan Fees	$	1,584
	Interest	$	63,860
	Funds earning credit	$	649,266
	Total	$	721,340
Expenses			
	Direct & Indirect	$	103,468
	FDIC Assesment	$	11,996
	Service center charges		
	Data Processing	$	9,676
	Deposit Ops	$	17,338
	Payment Processing	$	6,490
	Loan Operations	$	1,599
	Network	$	5,274
	Occupancy	$	10,903
	Interest Expense	$	220,741
	General Overhead	$	65,545
	Funds use charge	$	5,594
	Total	$	458,624
Net Profit		$	262,716
	Contribute to Loan Loss	$	1,710
Profit after LL		$	261,006

Seminole Region of Branches

BRANCH NAME >>	A	B	E	G	H	Total
Average Deposits	29,962,062	97,773,276	33,534,975	47,052,404	30,793,302	409,423,603
Avg Gross Loans	305,728	6,835,596	1,694,287	924,016	728,209	17,261,037
Income						
Interest Income	6,379	95,887	26,326	18,378	10,370	270,898
Non-Interest Income	25,877	93,530	62,673	62,658	40,063	498,617
Funds Earning Credit	250,192	816,396	280,019	392,880	257,112	3,418,589
Total	282,448	1,005,813	369,018	473,916	307,546	4,188,104
Expenses						
Salary and Benefits	50,571	109,391	80,270	67,664	49,656	572,091
Occupancy	8,982	38,992	15,657	17,327	39,880	163,597
FDIC Assessment	9,869	32,245	11,068	15,493	10,170	134,977
Other Direct and Indirect Expenses	15,971	28,367	14,865	20,012	16,316	157,565
Service Center Charges						
Retail Banking	-8,140	-22,171	-10,743	-10,475	-6,666	-101,930
Bank Services	6,806	18,533	8,983	8,760	5,571	85,222
Dealer Center	984	5,256	1,031	776	1,501	15,417
Loan Servicing	125	3,231	673	208	178	6,943
Special Credits	700	32,681	6,960	1,168	1,005	78,029
Core Processing	5,815	16,342	7,819	7,504	4,789	73,924
Item Processing	14,476	39,417	19,101	18,635	11,851	181,257
Network	2,830	4,717	2,359	3,774	4,246	32,078
Buildings	0	0	0	0	0	0
Interest Expense	110,572	304,750	124,760	183,485	93,488	1,389,373
General Overhead	58,518	148,694	85,954	85,495	82,981	726,672
Funds Use Charge	2,553	57,082	14,146	7,717	6,083	144,138
Total	280,631	817,528	382,903	427,543	321,049	3,659,352
Net Profit (Loss) Before Tax	1,817	188,285	-13,884	46,373	-13,503	528,752

Commercial Loan Profit Centers

BRANCH NAME >>	J	K	L	M	N	Total
Average Deposits	0	-224	0	0	0	-224
Avg Gross Loans	154,651,274	149,048,721	87,374,002	108,411,173	107,578,834	607,064,005
Income						
Interest Income	2,439,579	2,496,049	1,413,533	1,701,100	1,732,993	9,783,253
Non-Interest Income	33,244	22,474	-280	6,394	18,292	80,125
Funds Earning Credit	0	-2	0	0	0	-2
Total	2,472,823	2,518,521	1,413,253	1,707,494	1,751,285	9,863,376
Expenses						
Salary and Benefits	141,147	121,601	109,966	115,317	101,268	589,298
Occupancy	4,385	6,513	5,355	10,553	4,778	31,583
Occupancy	0	0	635	844	0	1,480
Other Direct and Indirect Expenses	150,530	134,350	113,885	127,157	102,672	628,594
FDIC Assessment	0	0	0	0	0	0
Other Direct and Indirect Expenses	9,383	12,750	3,919	11,841	1,404	39,296
Service Center Charges						
Retail Banking	0	0	0	0	0	0
Bank Services	0	0	0	0	0	0
Dealer Center	1,244	1,756	7,721	0	3,704	14,426
Loan Servicing	29,793	43,726	16,928	22,753	33,349	146,549
Special Credits	283,366	281,607	168,793	210,255	317,225	1,261,246
Core Processing	1,745	1,924	1,308	831	2,002	7,809
Item Processing	0	0	0	0	0	0
Network	4,246	3,774	2,830	2,830	2,359	16,039
Buildings	0	0	0	0	0	0
Interest Expense	0	0	0	0	0	0
General Overhead	104,282	100,235	86,178	95,072	79,135	464,901
Funds Use Charge	1,291,318	1,244,543	729,602	905,170	898,335	5,068,968
Total	1,870,909	1,818,428	1,132,600	1,374,622	1,443,557	7,640,115
Net Profit (Loss) Before Tax	601,914	700,093	280,653	332,872	307,728	2,223,260

CHAPTER 10

REVIEW WITH MANAGEMENT TEAM

The final step is discussion and decision making based on the Simplified Profitability results.

The chapter provides an agenda template, including potential performance improvement tactics that might be indicated.

Examples are included that show how the model information can be extended with the addition of key indicators and break-even analysis for each profit center.

The following is intended to be a suggested outline of a management presentation to the profit center managers by senior management. Of course the staff that developed and assembled the presentation actually does the explanation. However, it must come across that this is a program that comes from senior management.

Agenda

- CEO objectives
- Simplified Profitability
- Profit centers, service centers, general overhead centers
- Service centers charge outs (activity based)
- GOH allocation
- Funds transfer rate
- Profit center reports (individual & summary)
- Profit improvement focus
- Action plan (s)

  Operational:
    - Close unprofitable centers
    - Measure & improve staff productivity
    - Reduce *Hot Money*
    - Correct domicile of deposit balances
    - Address line item expenses

  Marketing:
    - Determine break even potential of loss centers
    - Evaluate traffic patterns, signage, access
    - Develop cross selling to existing customers

  Financial:
    - Sale & lease back of loss centers
    - Review prepaid & depreciation expense

- Project team recognition

Case History: Addition of key indicator and break-even analysis

The previous agenda was not meant to be so structured that creative additions could not integrated into the meeting. The following examples are the real value of a valid and Simplified Profitability System. The system should provide information appropriate to build *action plans* and for management to make decisions to improve profitability.

The first two illustrations show key indicators of the cost components of the profit centers at a bank. Two important indicators are occupancy and salaries with benefits expressed as a percentage of deposits.

- Occupancy expressed in basis points (bps) relative to deposits & compared to bank average
- Salary/Benefits expressed in basis points (bps) relative to deposits & compared to bank average

The graphs identify the *outliers* (the unusual variance from the average) that should be looked at more closely to understand that function and look for improvement.

The second illustration shows two branches with their present figures and the forecast figure given certain growth or reduction goals. These are expressed with three primary goals and the relative change is shown in the forecast column.

This can avoid the over-reaction of some that immediately want to slash costs or close an unprofitable branch. Many times, breakeven and better can be achieved with a very small improvement goal.

Key Indicator Report

Period 8,9,10-2012

Resp Center	ref	Balances Deposits	**Deposit Occupancy**	bp	avg bp
01	1	100,411,216	27,897.71	11.1	24.8
02	2	15,140,665	7,310.83	19.3	24.8
03	3	35,607,465	14,671.21	16.5	24.8
04	4	45,136,227	13,078.39	11.6	24.8
05	5	10,816,115	9,526.71	35.2	24.8
06	6	32,217,340	12,866.11	16.0	24.8
07	7	151,496,010	12,961.21	3.4	24.8
08	8	14,041,154	9,681.52	27.6	24.8
9	9	-	-		24.8
10	10	38,333,580	15,935.06	16.6	24.8
20	11	76,718,284	26,901.08	14.0	24.8
21	12	8,916,119	18,088.84	81.2	24.8
40	13	22,540,846	22,263.04	39.5	24.8
50	14	57,522,345	43,433.11	30.2	24.8
				322.2	
				24.8	

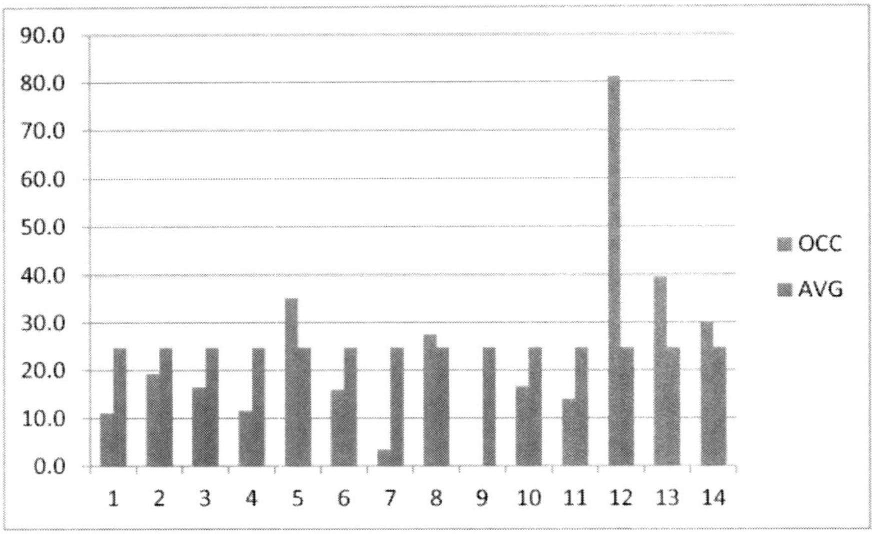

Key Indicator Report Period 8,9,10-2012

Resp Center	reference	Balances Deposits	**Salaries & Benefits**	bp	avg bp
01	1	100,411,216	155,839.49	62.1	74.4
02	2	15,140,665	34,646.00	91.5	74.4
03	3	35,607,465	62,615.91	70.3	74.4
04	4	45,136,227	59,542.79	52.8	74.4
05	5	10,816,115	30,959.00	114.5	74.4
06	6	32,217,340	50,992.00	63.3	74.4
07	7	151,496,010	89,568.65	23.6	74.4
08	8	14,041,154	27,542.00	78.5	74.4
	9		-		74.4
10	10	38,333,580	49,275.98	51.4	74.4
20	11	76,718,284	94,518.06	49.3	74.4
21	12	8,916,119	32,101.00	144.0	74.4
40	13	22,540,846	47,544.83	84.4	74.4
50	14	57,522,345	117,536.33	81.7	74.4
				967.4	
				74.4	

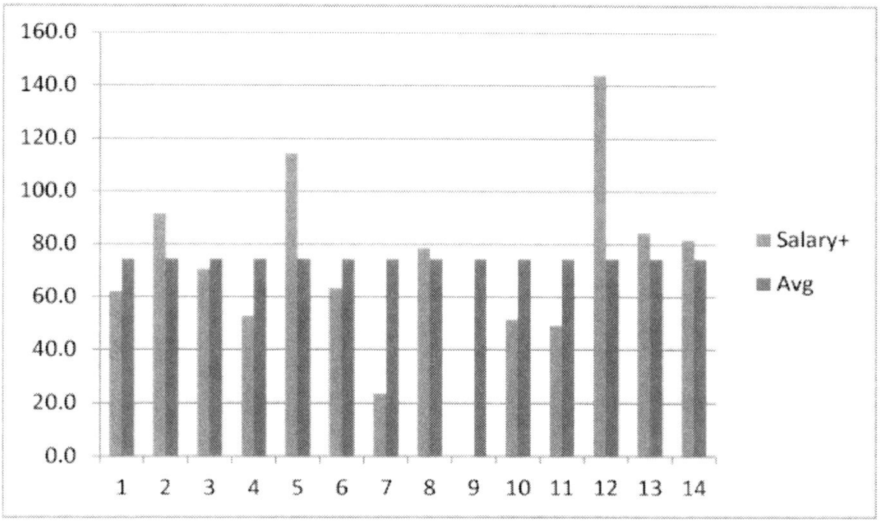

160.0
140.0
120.0
100.0
80.0
60.0
40.0
20.0
0.0
1 2 3 4 5 6 7 8 9 10 11 12 13 14
Salary+
Avg

The next two illustrations show two branches with their present figures and the forecast figure given certain growth or reduction goals. The objective here is to estimate the break- even levels to achieve profitability or see the impact of *what if* scenarios.

- Longwood branch- increase deposit & loans 10%, see resulting improvement

- Loxahatchee branch- increase deposits 5%, reduce controllable expenses 10%, achieve break even

In the examples there are three simple user inputs that cause the Profitability Report to change These are expressed with three primary goals and the relative change is shown in the forecast column. This can avoid the over-reaction of some that immediately want to slash cost or close an unprofitable branch. Many times the break even and better can be achieved with a very small and achievable improvement goal.

The models illustrated are very simple based on the Simplified Profitability reports. The user's imagination is the only limit to how complex this can become. A word to the wise, "keep it simple"!!

Branch Breakeven Analysis			**Bank XYZ**
		Forecast Change	
	Growth Goal for Deposits	10%	<<*user input*
	Growth Goal for Loans	10%	<<*user input*
	Goal for Comp,Occ,Dir, Ind	0%	<<*user input*
Branch	**Period**		
Longwood	QTR4-2012		Forecast Future Period
Total Deposits & Repos		22,540,846	24,794,931
Available Capital		1,282,842	1,282,842
Total Gross Loans		18,286,614	20,115,275
Income			
	Deposit & Interchange Fees	19,072	20,979
	Loan Fees	3,338	3,672
	Interest	232,056	255,262
	Funds earning credit	136,066	149,673
	Total	390,532	429,585
Expenses			
	Comp, Occup, Direct & Indirect	141,546	141,546
	FDIC Assesment	13,266	14,593
	Service center charges		
	Data Processing	3,820	4,202
	Deposit Ops	1,044	1,148
	Items Processing	2,195	2,415
	Electronic Payments	4,173	4,590
	Internet Banking	2,495	2,745
	Loan Operations	2,756	3,032
	Network	2,453	2,698
	Branch Admin	287	316
	Operations Admin	2,910	3,201
	Interest Expense	62,640	68,904
	General Overhead	42,645	42,645
	Funds use charge	104,442	114,886
	Total	386,672	406,920
Net Profit		3,860	22,665

Branch Breakeven Analysis | **Bank XYZ**

	Forecast Change	
Growth Goal for Deposits	5%	<<*user input*
Growth Goal for Loans	0%	<<*user input*
Goal for Comp,Occ,Dir, Ind	-10%	<<*user input*

Branch	**Period**			Forecast Future Period
Loxahatchee	QTR4-2012			
Total Deposits & Repos		$	15,140,665	15,897,699
Available Capital		$	861,684	861,684
Total Gross Loans		$	11,846	11,846
Income				
	Deposit & Interchange Fees	$	40,081	42,085
	Loan Fees	$	24	24
	Interest	$	95	95
	Funds earning credit	$	91,395	95,965
	Total	$	131,595	138,169
Expenses				
	Comp, Occup, Direct & Indirect	$	51,761	46,585
	FDIC Assesment	$	9,114	9,570
	Service center charges			
	Data Processing	$	5,165	5,424
	Deposit Ops	$	1,690	1,775
	Items Processing	$	3,631	3,813
	Electronic Payments	$	6,904	7,249
	Internet Banking	$	3,374	3,543
	Loan Operations	$	-	-
	Network	$	1,090	1,145
	Branch Admin	$	388	408
	Operations Admin	$	3,935	4,132
	Interest Expense	$	34,569	36,297
	General Overhead	$	18,111	18,111
	Funds use charge	$	68	68
	Total	$	139,802	138,119
Net Profit		$	(8,207)	50

CHAPTER 11

SUMMARY - WORK PLAN EXAMPLE

The author has given many public presentations and has experienced the same occasional feedback from audiences as other public speakers. The audience wants to thank you for a great idea or insight but wonders why you didn't tell them specific steps to accomplish the objective or implement the idea. Well, usually there isn't enough time. (Or you don't want to give away trade secrets.)

In this Chapter we will try to summarize everything we have discussed in the form of a generic work plan. You will have to modify or customize it for the individual situation. However, don't change it too much and expect the same results. Remember the popular TV show where they say, "Don't try this at home!"

Authors note: Each step relates to a particular step in the chapters in the book. Just refer to the table of contents.

ORGANIZATION COST / PROFITABILITY ANALYSIS

Start with an overview of the system. Review the initial planning phase. Buy-in and leadership starts at the "C" level - CEO, COO, CFO, CLO, CIO, etc.

Communicate the work plan objective to implement organization profitability reporting. Here are the steps:

1. Cost Accounting Concepts - Initial introduction of project to responsibility center managers.

Overview total system. Identify issues. Complete preliminary information request. Validate database as it exists. Select analysts.

2. Announce analysts at kick off meeting with senior management. Give overview of project.

This typically identifies a person(s) who can do all of the detail research, follow the approved work plan, develop and organize the appropriate intermediate and final presentation. This is usually someone from accounting who has access to many data sources. However, analysts have come from many ranks, i.e., audit, operations, etc. The analysts must be able to spend approximately 30 – 50% of their time on the project if it is to be completed in 3 to 4 months.

3. Determine responsibility centers.

This includes the definition of all responsibility centers, including new centers that may need to be setup in the accounting systems. These are then further classified as to profit center, service center and general overhead. This requires a review of the general ledger departmentalization.

Develop a design of the bank's general ledger to achieve department income & expense reporting, performance reporting (budget vs. actual), and unit cost/profitability analysis. (The unit will be a responsibility center.)

4. Document appropriate processes.

This addresses departments (service centers) that perform support functions to multiple profit centers. It could be a deposit operations service center that performs some functions for the loan profit center. It could be a branch that performs both deposit and loan functions.

A Work Distribution Chart is an excellent tool to measure and document this. Do not seek to identify each weekly effort because of variations by week. It is more appropriate to measure a typical week or month. It is easier and more accurate where the profit centers and service centers (departments) are aligned with the profit centers that will ultimately be measured for profitability.

5. Develop charge techniques. (Data processing important.)

For a bank that has a service bureau the monthly invoice is the key. The invoice probably has ancillary services such as a report writer, special services above account processing. An invoice has the count and charge for account processing for loans and deposits. Some may also charge for general ledger accounts. A typical technique is to take the total invoice and divide by the number of loan and deposit accounts (activity) to determine a cost per account.

For a bank that has account processing in-house, determine the total cost of account processing. This includes staff, equipment, maintenance, software depreciation, etc. This could be multiple departments. Then go to friends (other bankers who have service bureaus) and determine the *market rate* for loan and deposit accounts. (This could be a composite of several.)

Extend the banks' number of loan and deposit accounts by the *market rate*. The greatest majority of banks find that the resulting number recovered is less than the initial market rate value. This is called simulation and under-recovery. Adjust the market rate until a fair amount is recovered, i.e., adjusted market rate and actual rate are the same.

6. Segregate main office.

Few, if any, main office branches are completely free standing buildings with <u>no other</u> operations, overhead, or other profit centers (Trust, Investments, Loan origination) within their walls. The total occupancy costs usually result in a single figure (it could be a sum) that defines all occupancy expense. It probably includes heating and air conditioning the common areas.

The easiest way is to find some blueprints of the shared building(s) and determine the area (square feet) for each responsibility center. Otherwise, actual measurements must be made. A spreadsheet can be developed to charge each user (profit center, service center, or general overhead) for their share of the total cost of occupancy based on square footage (activity) required for that function.

7. Define cost accounting terms.

Most bankers think in terms of cost as two tiers, *fixed* and *variable*. Sometimes this is referred to as *direct* and *indirect*. Many FASB opinions are expressed in that manner. FASB 91 is a case in point. A more workable and accurate approach is to go to the Cost Accounting Handbook or an old cost accounting text from college days.

This author submits that the appropriate approach is a three tiered approach, direct, indirect, and general overhead. It is sometimes referred to as variable, variable overhead, and fixed overhead. This facilitates the measurement of direct and indirect and the appropriate grouping of general overhead in order to accomplish a *fully burdened* cost accounting system that can be balanced to the general ledger.

8. Determine base period.

The objective of the system is to determine the actual cost and profitability of an organization that is fully burdened in a specified period and balanced to the general ledger. This period can be one month, two months or a quarter. It is important to determine the actual cost before attempting to determine what it should cost. Actual cost of a specified period can be accomplished in a three month time frame. (Before things can change too much.)

9. Senior Management meeting - definitions, progress.

Don't wait until the last minute and spring things on senior management. Quite often they will have valuable input, especially with regard to profit center definition.

10. Define income accounting, classify income and expense; direct and indirect.

Income is typically more difficult to classify than expenses. Care should be taken to make sure that income figures are not just as of month-end but include any closing adjustments. In one client we found that 11% of income was adjusted. Needless to say this was an opportunity for improvement.

Many fees for deposit service are often not charged to the branch. One answer is to credit this income to deposit operations and reduce the expense that will be charged to the branch.

11. Develop base period amounts - direct, indirect, general overhead.

This task depends on the detail of charging departments in the general ledger. Sometimes it is necessary to go to human resources in order to get the detail necessary for payroll and fringe benefits. There is usually a hidden monster, a miscellaneous responsibility center called *overhead unallocated* or some similar name. Quite often it is necessary to dig into the accounts payable system to actually determine where these expenses should be charged for the base period. Obviously, more detail and accurate charging is required for the future.

12. Classify general overhead.

Depending on the detail in the general ledger and payroll system this can be relatively simple. It includes such things as executive expense, director's fees, legal fees (not loan related), human resources, finance & accounting, marketing. (Except where advertising can be identified by loan or deposit.)

13. Develop GOH allocation alternatives.

The author has never had a problem explaining to a president that someone has to pay for his or her salary. Likewise for other general overhead. The trick is to determine a fair way to allocate this amount to each of the profit centers. The author has seen some pretty wild schemes over the years.

The most accepted method over the past years has been to aggregate general overhead into one figure. Then, allocate overhead only to profit centers and for every dollar of non interest expense incurred in the profit center, a proportionate amount of general overhead is applied. Example: $0.25 of general overhead per $1.00 of non-interest direct & indirect expense.

14. Senior Management meeting - GOH allocation, progress.

Again, keep senior management informed and involved. Quite often they will have valuable input, especially with regard to general overhead allocation.

15. & 16. Develop "true" cost of funds, funds earning credit and funds use charge.

The author has heard many arguments for multiple pools of funds where someone is trying to apply asset/liability duration concepts rather than actual cost accounting. After many arguments we have found the use of a single pool of funds based on average cost and including the *cost to secure* works best the first time around.

Sometimes, clients have made some modifications to this when going into product cost accounting, but always tied back to the single pool in aggregate.

17. Senior Management meeting - policies summary, progress, internal funds transfer pricing.

By this time senior management should really be interested and a good conversation about the internal funds transfer rate should ensue.

18. Assemble profitability analysis.

18.1. Profit center results are produced.

18.2. Prepare management presentation - Reports are prepared and opportunities for improvement are identified.

The RMA Excel model can facilitate this. The most common question is, "How long does it take?" That depends on the number of responsibility centers. For an average community bank (less than $400 million) it might take 2 to 3 days the first time. Thereafter, the work takes less than a half day per period. A quarter is recommended as the period for profitability analysis.

The author has one client that loads the model and balances in less than 15 minutes. It all depends on how the general ledger is set up.

19. Management presentation.

- Profitability analysis
- Profit improvement strategy
- Plan continuing/expanded program

Activity Based

www.SimplifiedProfitability.com

APPENDIX

This Appendix includes three resources:

1. Glossary
2. The Factory Analogy
3. A General Ledger Responsibility Center Conceptual Design

Go to www.SimplifiedProfitability.com for additional information.

GLOSSARY

Activity-based costing (ABC) - A costing methodology that identifies activities in an organization and assigns the cost of each activity with resources, including time/salary, to all products and services according to the actual consumption by each unit produced.

Allocate - A subjective method to apportion or charge a particular expense or income for a specific purpose, or to particular products or organizations.

Analyst - Typically this is a person assigned to a special project to do the detail research, follow the work plan developed with management and organize the appropriate presentations.

Balance to the general ledger – To compare the results of a cost accounting and profitability system to the general ledger of the bank. The bank consolidated income before taxes reported to shareholders or regulators for the period is equal to the same bank total line of the Simplified Profitability system with no *dummy* products or *dummy* profit centers, or **Plug** accounts, within an acceptable margin of error, usually 1% or less.

Borrowed funds - Liabilities borrowed from another source other than depositors. It can be a temporary situation or long term. Funds borrowed for arbitrage are separated from short term borrowings.

Charge out - To apportion a specific expense from one responsibility center to a particular product or to another responsibility center based on a chosen *driver*. (Unit of measure.)

Close out - In cost accounting a closeout is the act of charging out all cost within a responsibility center, or cost center, and recording or adding them in another responsibility center(s).

Direct expense - Expenses clearly traceable to products or services that can be measured by count or by time. They vary directly with volume. Examples: Tellers, forms, new accounts, service centers such as data processing, loan operations, deposit operations, etc.

Fully burdened cost & profitability - The state of an organizational, product, customer, or relationship profitability model that logically assigns all **actual** direct and variable costs, indirect, and general overhead, with direct and assigned revenue.

Funds pricing - The price or rate assigned to or negotiated for an earning asset (loan) that generates interest income.

Funds transfer rate - The rate assigned to give credit to fund suppliers (deposits) and charge funds users (loans, investments)

General Overhead - Expenses that are a cost of doing business. They are fixed in nature and not traceable to products; defined in the general ledger. They should be allocated as a group. Examples: The board of directors, C level executives, finance, accounting, human resources, marketing, etc.

General overhead center - A responsibility center whose work supports all the cost centers and profits centers; defined in the general ledger.

Incremental cost - Any cost that is less than a *fully burdened cost*. It most commonly identifies variable (direct) cost only.

Indirect expense - Expenses incurred in delivering products and traceable only to product groups; defined in the general ledger. Examples: Branch occupancy, telephone, utilities, branch administration, etc.

Matched funds - A term related to asset liability management systems or loan pricing systems. The intent is to match terms of funds supply products with terms of funds use products, with the theoretical goal of minimizing yield curve risk.

Multiple pools of funds - A bank may choose to establish multiple pools of funds where there is a large market and interest costs of money, competitive rates, vary significantly between geographic funds supply markets. It occurs on the funds use side where the bank chooses to charge different rates for groups of asset products such as investments, commercial loans, and can also be affected by variations in geographic competition.

Net supplier of funds - When an organization (branch) has more deposit balances than loan balances.

Net user of funds - When an organization (branch) has more loan balances than deposit balances.

Over-recover - When a cost accounting/profitability system model produces more income, expense, or profitability for a specific responsibility center or the bank in whole than the general ledger.

Peg rate - The aggregate rate of all funds supply sources which is used as an aggregate rate for all funds users. It is a single rate that is the fulcrum of the funds transfer rate.

Period - A month, quarter, or any specific calendar series of months. Within this period all actual data is converted into a profitability system as it actually is.

Plug - This is a slang term used to describe a misleading practice applied to *force balance* the monetary amounts of two systems when reconciliation does not indicate equality. The out of balance condition is resolved by posting the difference, or adjustment, in a miscellaneous account.

Profit center - A responsibility center which generates income by selling a product(s) or performing a service, with the goal of creating a profit contribution to the bank.

Sequential close outs - See close out; when one center closes out to others, then that receiving center in turn closes out to another. That is a sequential close out. This can go on with many close outs occurring in sequence.

Service center - A responsibility center whose duty is to provide service in the operation of profit centers. The costs a service center incurs are charged to all responsibility centers it services based on activity drivers.

Single pool of funds - All sources of funds are aggregated into one pool of funds. All funds users draw from and are charged for using this pool of funds.

Standard cost format - This format uses three tiers of cost, direct, indirect, and general overhead. (See glossary.) It is not necessary to develop a *standard*. The actual cost can be display in a three tier format. **It is what it is!**

True Cost of Funds - This is the total market cost of money (interest) plus the direct, indirect, and general overhead cost of all the branches to secure and service those deposits. Each component and the total are expressed as percentages.

Under-recover - When a cost accounting/profitability system produces less income, expense, or profitability of a specific responsibility center, or the bank in total than the general ledger actual results.

APPENDIX - FACTORY ANALOGY

Illustration: Manufacturing Analogy

Simplified Profitability is built on a solid foundation; cost accounting best practices adapted from industrial engineering for banking. This is especially apparent in the determination of funds transfer rates.

Here is a manufacturing factory analogy, an easy to understand mental model. Please refer to the Factory diagram. This left to right process diagram is a high-level value stream flow.

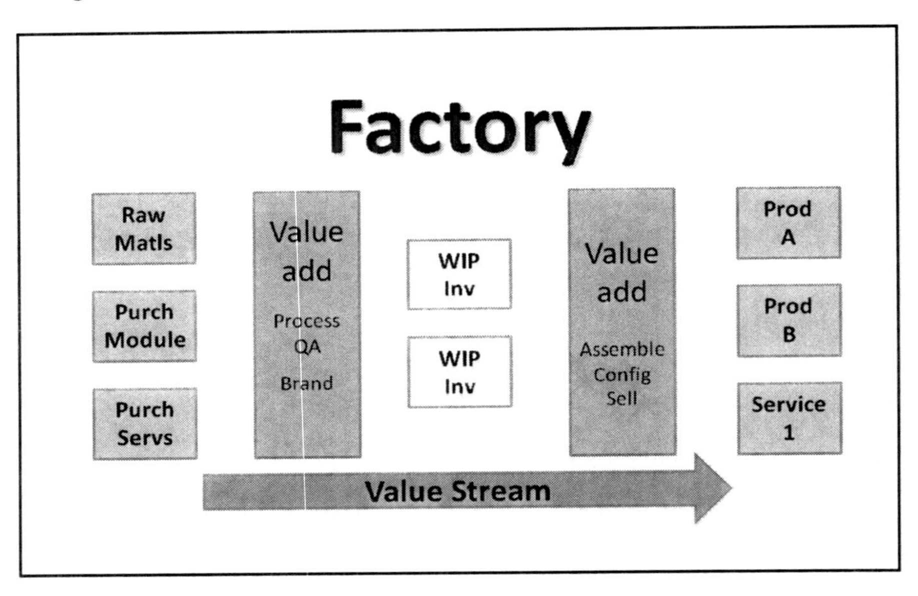

Factory

At the beginning of the process, on the left side, you can see the inputs: raw materials, purchased modules and subassemblies, and purchased services. In this hypothetical factory the first group of value-add processes and quality assurance translate those raw materials, services and subassemblies into Work in Process inventory, WIP, the boxes in the middle of the diagram.

The second group of value-add processes includes the steps to assemble, configure, market and sell the finished goods, the products and services, to meet market demand. In this analogy there are two very distinct value-add process groups:

1. Creation of the intermediate working process inventory.
2. The assembly that pulls together WIP components and services to meet market demand.

Financial Institution

The second figure translates this manufacturing illustration into the financial institution process. On the far left we see that deposits, borrowings and purchased services are similar to raw materials and purchased subassemblies in manufacturing. The first value-add process group creates a pool of funds and services for a financial institution. You can see that the functions of the branches in new account opening,

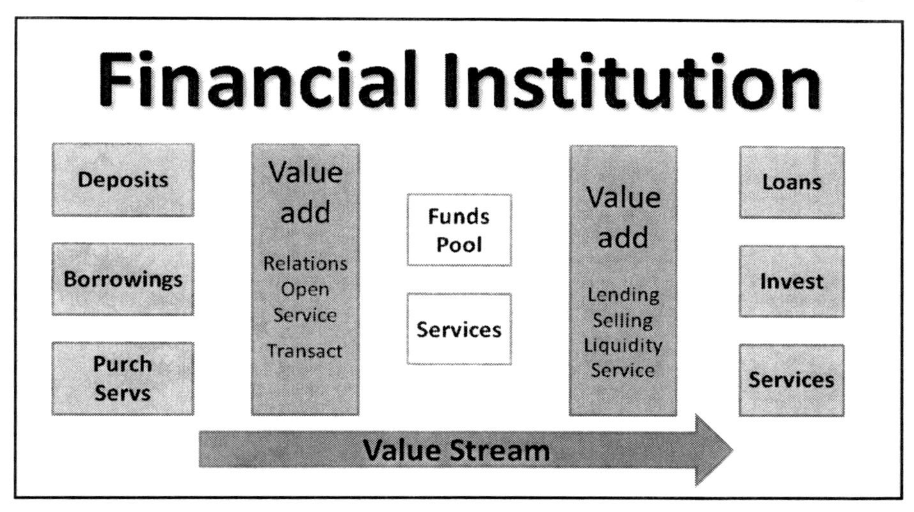

customer relationships, and transaction processing are comparable to creating WIP inventory.

The second value-add block on the right uses the funds pool, through underwriting, competition, and liquidity requirements, and so on, to produce to the market demand for loans and investment needs. And, of course, financial institutions have for many years resold and added value to purchased services for their customers.

Valuation of work-in-process inventory is critical in managing a factory, and it is just as important that a financial institution value the funds pool based on their value-add processes plus the external costs of deposits, borrowings and purchased services.

In the Simplified Profitability model this valuation happens in the Funds Transfer Rate worksheet. See the example in Chapter 7, page 71.

This worksheet accomplishes the inventory valuation of the raw materials and the initial value-add of a financial institution. In the factory analogy diagram it brings us through the first three major steps, to the funds pool, the box in the middle of the factory analogy diagram. Just as shown in the flow chart, in this worksheet we include the direct and indirect costs, and the general overhead associated with these first stage value-added functions.

GENERAL LEDGER RESPONSIBILITY CENTER DEFINITION EXAMPLE

In many RMA consulting engagements that deal with evaluation of in-house core processing vs. outsource core processing it is the first time banks have seen our metric; cost per account per month. It may be their first exposure to a practical activity based unit cost method. This sometimes leads them to ask how their general ledger could be re-structured.

The following diagram is a conceptual example of a general ledger design for a bank with centralized service centers such as core processing, items processing, deposit operations, and loan operations charging out to profit centers that use those services. This is an essential foundation for a fully burdened profitability center system.

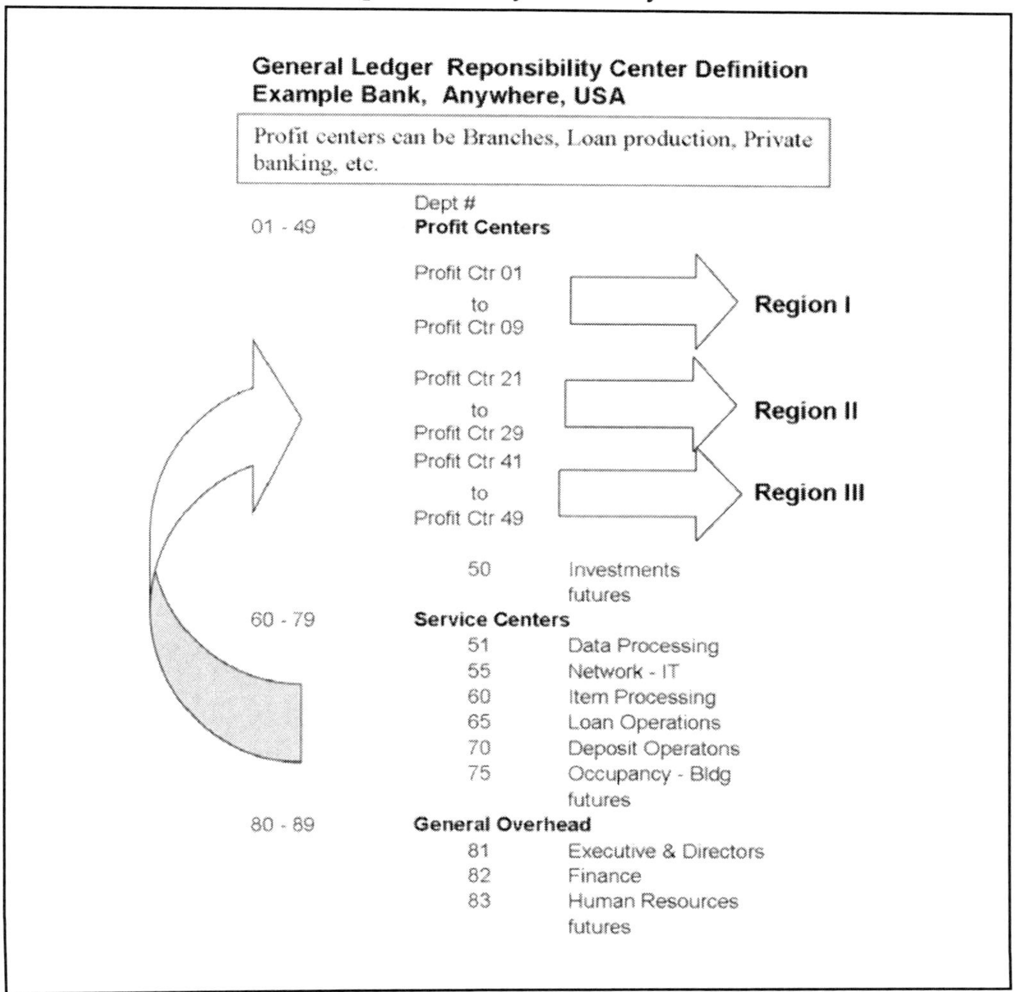

CPSIA information can be obtained at www.ICGtesting.com
Printed in the USA
LVOW110144100513

333047LV00001B/4/P

9 780988 474604